FROM CRYSTAL TO SMOKE
A THEATER PLAY

*English translation by ESKA Publishing and Katrin Holt, Lily Heise,
Arnold Gremy and Paul and Jack Lipscomb.
A special thanks to Katrin Holt, Lily Heise, Arnold Gremy and
Paul and Jack Lipscomb for their editing support.
Published with the support of CNL – National Book Center – Paris.*

© 2010 ESKA PUBLISHING WASHINGTON – EDITIONS ESKA PARIS
for the Publisher Consultant Paul Lipscomb
3808 SW Dosch Road, Portland, Oregon, 97239 - USA
paullips3@gmail.com

ISBN 978-2-7472-1544-2

Distribution World Wide:
ESKA Publishing
12, rue du Quatre-Septembre
75002 Paris - France
Tel: +33 (0)1 42 86 55 65
Fax: +33 (0)1 42 60 45 35
http://www.eska.fr

Distribution in North America:
IPM: International Publishers Marketing
22841 Quicksilver Drive, Dulles, VA 20166
USA
Tel: 703-661-1531
Fax: 703-661-1547
www.internationalpublishermarket.com

Printed in Canada by Transcontinental

Jacques Attali

FROM CRYSTAL TO SMOKE

A THEATER PLAY

This play tells the story of a secret meeting, as close to historical reality as possible, held amongst the main Nazi leaders on the morning of November 12, 1938 in Berlin, two days after Crystal Night. The Final Solution came from this gathering, well before the Wansee conference that took place on January 20, 1942.

Several shorthand typists, including Dr Fritz Dörr, took down the exchanges. At the end of the war, Fritz Dörr handed his notes, a partial account of the meeting, over to the Americans. Those notes were used at the Nuremberg trials. Those of the other shorthand typists, containing half of the meeting, were never found.

The document was then sent to the German Archives (reference number "PS-1816"[1]). In 1998, Jewish families, heirs to insurance policies never honoured by the Nazi State referred the case to the State of California in order to discover some evidence of the collaboration of insurance companies with the Nazi government. Risk International, hired by the State of California to conduct this investigation (with the support of Avotaynu as part of the Living Heirs Project), contacted the German insurance company Allianz and traced back the document.

This play is inspired by the partial *verbatim* of the meeting and by the first-hand accounts provided by various participants including Bernhard Lösener from the department of Jewish Affairs at the Ministry of the Interior, and Ernst Wörman, through Professor Gerald D. Feldman's book *(Allianz and the German Insurance Business, 1933-1945,* Cambridge University Press, 2001), and through the research of Allianz group historians under the supervision of Barbara Eggenkämper, whom I thank for their support. I am also indebted to Professor Edouard Husson for his careful rereading of this text.

The title given to this play echoes that of the fundamental biology book by Henri Atlan, *Le Cristal et la Fumée,* published at the Éditions du Seuil I 1978.

CHARACTERS:

Bürckel, Joseph, (43 years old): Gauleiter of Austria.

Daluege, Kurt (41 years old): Himmler's Deputy, Lieutenant General of the SS Police, commander of the Order Police.

Frick, Wilhelm (61 years old): Minister of the Interior from 1933.

Funk, Walter (48 years old): Minister of the Economy, after his position as Goebbels' State Secretary of the Ministry for Propaganda.

Goebbels, Joseph (41 years old): Minister of Propaganda.

Göring, Hermann (45 years old): Number 2 of the regime, field marshal, in charge of the Four Year Plan and preparation for the war.

Gürtner, Franz (57 years old): Minister of Justice from 1933.

Heydrich, Reinhard (34 years old): Himmler's Deputy, head of the SS.

Hilgard, Edouard (54 years old): Managing Director of Allianz and president of the Federation of German Insurance Companies.

Himmler, Heinrich (38 years old): SS Reichsfürher, controls the police, Gestapo, SS and SD.

Kehrl, Hans (39 years old): Göring's right-hand man, head of the Planning Bureau for the Ministry of the Economy.

Von Krosigk, Count Lutz Schwerin Von, (43 years old): Minister of Finance from 1932.

Wörmann, Ernst (54 years old): State Secretary of Political Affairs at the Ministry of Foreign Affairs.

PROLOG

A cinema screen (the rest of the scene is in darkness).

Off-screen voice, spoken over news images:

On the June 9, 1938, the Führer, who had just succeeded in occupying Austria, has had the Berlin synagogue destroyed, due to it being *"too close to the House of German Art"*. At an international conference in Evian in July, Germany requested, without success, that France, Great Britain, the United States and other democracies take in the German Jews whom it is set on expelling. All countries either refuse or only agree to take in very small groups. On August 10, the Nuremberg synagogue is destroyed by looters. At the beginning of September, the Führer encourages the Sudeten Germans to revolt against the Czechoslovakian government, and then annexes the region to Germany. This annexation is approved by the French and the British on September 30 in Munich, hoping that it will avoid war from breaking out.

On the October 28, 17,000 Polish Jews, who had taken refuge in Germany in 1914, are sent back to Poland by Hitler and refused entry, leaving them stuck in a no man's land between the two countries.

In Paris, on Monday November 7, the son of one of these Polish Jewish refugees, Herschel Grynszpan, shoots the first diplomat whom he comes across in the Reich's Embassy, Ernst Vom Rath, seriously injuring him. Grynszpan is arrested by the French police who later hand him over to the Nazis.

On Tuesday November 8, Hitler arrives in Munich to celebrate the 15th anniversary of his failed coup d'état of November 9, 1923, as he does every year, with all of his lieutenants. After hearing about the attack in Paris, he sends his personal doctor to Vom Rath's bedside.

At the end of the afternoon on Wednesday November 9, Vom Rath dies from his injuries. At 7 pm, Hitler learns of his death in Munich and gives Goebbels the order to *"not stand in the way of spontaneous acts"* against Jews. At eight o'clock in the evening, Goebbels attributes the assassination of Vom Rath to *"the worldwide Jewish community"*, and denounces a *"Jewish conspiracy against Germany"*, asking the German population to demonstrate against the Jews.

At 1:20 am on Thursday November 10, Heydrich, on the Führer's orders transmitted by Goebbels, authorises Gestapo leaders to disguise themselves in plain clothes, set fire to synagogues, destroy Jewish shop windows and to arrest *"as many Jews (men, not too old and in good health,) as the concentration camps could hold"*. Heydrich orders his troops to ensure that the fires do not spread beyond Jewish properties, to make sure that the non-Jewish businesses are protected from any attacks, and to forbid pillaging. Each local section of the party wants to organise its own pogrom and figure on the list of achievements of what would straight away become known on the streets of Berlin as "Crystal Night".

In total, several hundred synagogues are set alight; 7,500 shops are destroyed, almost all of the Jewish cemeteries are desecrated; at least 91 Jews are killed; 30,000 others are arrested and sent to Dachau.

On the morning of the 10th, the Jews have to clear up the broken glass scattered across the sidewalks and conceal the gaping shop fronts with boards. Notices appear everywhere in Germany advertising, *"Shop for rent immediately", "Shop already sold to Aryans"*. On that morning, Jewish pupils are no longer permitted to enter elementary and high schools, and universities. Goebbels gives the order for demonstrations to stop and tells the press that he has had no part in them: *"Imagine what the reaction against the Jews would have been if we had organized it"*. At midday, Göring leaves Munich for Berlin, after having seen Hitler again. At 8pm, all the Reich's radio stations re-broadcast Göring's call requesting that an end be put to the "spontaneous phase" of the anti-Jewish action.

On Friday November 11, the United States, France and Great Britain celebrate their 1918 victory and meekly protest against Crystal Night. Roosevelt calls back his ambassador from Berlin. The French and British ones remain at their posts. During the day, Göring spends a considerable amount of time on the telephone with Hitler, who stayed in Munich. The anti-Jewish demonstrations slow down, and then come to a halt.

At 11am on Saturday November 12, Göring summons all the barons of Nazism, some of whom were with him in Munich only the day before, and a number of senior Nazi officials to a large meeting room adjacent to his office, situated in the Ministry of Air that he has just had built as the government's command centre.

The screen disappears. The curtain is raised revealing a large meeting room with fourteen seats and three doors, a U-shaped table, and another table with coffee and cups. Some maps are scattered about. On the wall, there is a huge portrait of Hitler. There is a telephone on a table in the background.

The Nazi officials enter one after another. They greet each other with military or civil salutes, talk quietly amongst themselves, take their seats, and observe each other. Their gestures and twitches must be understood as signs of their ranks, their clannishness, their hatred and their streak of madness.

The off-screen voice starts again, announcing the names of those entering.

Dr Goebbels, Minister of propaganda; Walter Funk, Minister of the Economy; Count Schwerin Von Krosigk, Minister of Finance; Wilhelm Frick, Minister of the Interior; Hans Gürtner, Minister of Justice; Heinrich Himmler, head of the SS and his two deputies: Reinhard Heydrich, head of the Security Police and General Daluege, head of the Order Police; Dr Ernst Wörmann, State Secretary at the Ministry of Foreign Affairs; Joseph Bürckel, head of the party in Austria; Marshal Hermann Göring, number 2 of the regime, and his advisor, Hans Kehrl, head of the Economic Planning Bureau.

Kehrl is carrying files and around fifteen copies of a text that he hands over to Göring before sitting next to him. Göring is in the centre. Goebbels, Himmler, and Heydrich are to his right. To his left, between Goebbels and himself, one chair remains empty.

ACT I

GÖRING

Please sit down, gentlemen. Heil Hitler, Heil Hitler. Today's meeting is of great importance. M. Kehrl, please note down everything. Well, everything... I'll tell you when something does not need to be noted... Silence, please. Take your seats. Hurry up! *(He whispers to Himmler who is sitting next to him)* It's a nice room, isn't it? Well suited for an important meeting like this. Very well suited. I designed everything myself. The chairs, the tables the wallpaper ... Alright, hurry up. No, leave that chair empty (*the chair next to him*). Is everyone here? Silence! ...

After the events of two days ago, we cannot allow the situation to worsen. We cannot accept this anarchy anymore! You must realise that we are potentially on the brink of war. We must concentrate all of our energies in order to produce what we will need to win. And the Jewish issue must not interfere with our military preparations. A very comprehensive and coherent strategy must be defined regarding the Jews, so that they are no longer in our way when war breaks out. And we will not achieve this with your demonstrations, dear Goebbels. I just received a note from our Führer's secretary, Martin Bormann, passing on the order for me to sort out the Jewish issue, by any means necessary.

The Führer has already given me this order himself in greater detail this morning by telephone, and he also explained it to me the day before yesterday in Munich. He has entrusted me with the mission of coordinating all actions carried out against the Jews. All of them. And I have gathered you here this morning to give you my instructions on this subject... To begin with, here is a..... Dr Himmler?

HIMMLER

Marshal, I assume your mission is to coordinate the economic side of things! I oversee police action and propaganda. And I would like to remind you that I only report to the Führer. I have come to this meeting to listen to you, nothing more.

GOEBBELS

I'm very sorry but propaganda is answerable to my Ministry! And the Führer...

GÖRING

Ah, let's not start like that! This is neither the place, nor the time, gentlemen, to settle your bickering over jurisdiction. We will speak about that later. Goebbels, Himmler, I'll keep you both at the end of this meeting at which, need I remind you, all of our government leaders are present... Not only our closest friends..... Am I making myself clear? Even for you, Dr Goebbels? Mr Heydrich? General Daluege? Good. Let's begin.

We are here to solve the Jewish problem, and it is mainly economic. Naturally, measures will need to be taken by the Minister of Police, Mr Himmler, and by his two deputies, also present here today, Mr Daluege and Mr Heydrich, who get on famously with one another and work extremely well together... The Minister of Propaganda, Mr Goebbels, and the Minister of the Interior Mr Frick, just like each and every one of you in this room, will have a role to play, as you will see shortly.... We will also look at how the Austrians are dealing with this issue. And they are dealing with it particularly well, so it would seem. Bravo Mr Bürckel, as Gauleiter of Austria, you seem to be doing a good job. Which does not surprise me in the slightest as you Austrians have known how to bring inferior populations to heel since the Hapsburgs! That is why I have asked you to come, so that you could enlighten us with your advice.

BÜRCKEL

Thank you Marshal, and I...

GÖRING

Don't thank me too soon... Alright, let's get started. In order to solve the Jewish issue once and for all, I have had my services prepare a draft decree with the assistance of the Minister of Justice, Mr Gürtner, present here, and whose abilities I admire. Recently, he has shown his skills again by requesting that his judges be justly lenient towards some members of our party who have proved themselves to be... let's say... particularly aggressive towards Jews... Here, read this.

Göring passes copies of the text sitting in front of him around the room.

17

HIMMLER

Yet another piece of paper! We just keep meeting to go over texts! That's not how we will manage to finish off the Jews. We have to kick them out of the country, it's as simple as that, kick them out! And if they do not go, there should be other means of getting rid of them. We do not need a "text" for that.

GÖRING

I am of the same opinion. Our civil servants have already devised great plans during countless meetings over the course of the past five years. None of the plans has been carried out. The Jews are still here to ridicule us. They work, stroll around, take the train, go to the theatre and to the cinema! They still own businesses, housing, factories and shops. We have to get rid of them methodically, scientifically and not by using mindless force - like what happened the day before yesterday, Dr Goebbels - which has backfired on us. We are therefore going to aryanize the German economy, exclude Jews and get them out of our sight.

GOEBBELS

But, Marshal, that was exactly the aim of the demonstrations the day before yesterday; to make life impossible for them, so that they would leave.

GÖRING

But they are still here! Five years after we came to power! Mr Stuckart, as a State Secretary, you are Mr Frick's deputy, at the Ministry of the Interior, you are the expert in such matters. Remind us how many Jews are still in Germany?

FRICK

Approximately 400 000, four fifths of those who were here in 1933.

HIMMLER

Do you realise that! Four fifths! We have only made a fifth of them leave, which is about 2,000 per month! In five years! That's a terrible failure. And what about the crossbreeds? Are you including them in your figures?

FRICK

The half-Jews? No, I'd like to remind you that they are not Jewish according to the laws of 1933. We had thus decided to maintain their Germanic origins.

GÖRING

That wasn't the best idea we've had! Yes... well, what's done is done. Mr. Wörmann, your Ministry, Foreign Affairs, doesn't seem to be succeeding in finding a dumping ground to dispose of our Jews?

WÖRMANN

Marshal, it is not our fault no one wants them! Of the 300,000 Jews who requested an American visa, only 30,000 managed to obtain one! The Dutch, Belgians, Swiss, French and British have also closed their borders to them. Canada's Prime Minister has just announced that "none" was still "too many".

GÖRING

It shouldn't be difficult to find at least one country where they could be crammed. It doesn't need to be heaven on earth.

HIMMLER

Our diplomats cannot achieve the impossible. We aren't the only ones wanting to see an end to the Jews. All of Europe, even France, is demonstrating against them. In the United States, the press approves of what we are doing, but no one wants Jews in their country.

GÖRING

The democrats have understood that we want the Jews to go and make a nuisance of themselves elsewhere.

WÖRMANN

In fact, no one wants to see moneyless Jews arrive in their country.

HIMMLER

The rich ones will just have to pay for the poor to leave then!

GÖRING

Well, the problem is that even the rich don't want to leave without their money. And as our marks are worthless abroad, they want to change them for foreign currencies before leaving. And it is out of the question that we let the Jews leave with our foreign currency! We therefore have to find foreign Jews who can finance the conversion of our Jews' assets with their currency. I have met at least two: Raltenberg, a Dane, and Dubler, an American, who were prepared to organise this financial deal. I told them that we would be forced to find other solutions to the Jewish problem if they didn't get the money together quickly. But, they haven't been able to find the money.

VON KROSIGK

The American Jews want it to go through their government, but Roosevelt refuses because he neither wants to provide us with the currency nor take in the Jews.

GÖRING

And yet they should go! Wherever that may be, it isn't our problem. Even to the moon! To a place where they will be unable to harm us, where they will die quickly, forgotten, like, Ecuador, Colombia, Venezuela or Madagascar. Ah, if only we, like Stalin, had the accommodating Siberian steppes....

GOEBBELS

Send them anywhere, except to Palestine which is a Jewish state, like the British are currently suggesting with the Peel Commission report. This could be dangerous for us as they could cut off our oil route. Madagascar would be the best solution. They wouldn't last long there.

HEYDRICH

In the meantime, we can use them here as hostages, as a security and bargaining counters.

GÖRING

No, we have no need of them! We have to find a final and conclusive solution. Germany should become hell on earth for them!

DALLUEGE

Why not just kill them?

Göring signals him to keep quiet.

HIMMLER

We shouldn't have to come across them everywhere! I have my own idea about that and I…

GÖRING

We are gathered here to eradicate Jews from the German economy and subject them to my authority.

HEYDRICH

To the Führer's authority...

GÖRING

To my authority: the Führer has entrusted me with the mission of coordinating all action carried out against the Jews.

GOEBBELS

And driving them out was exactly the reason why the Führer allowed me to... follow "Crystal Night:" mobilized people have pushed the Jews out.

GÖRING (*giving Goebbels a cruel look*)

"Mobilized".... Let's talk about that! I am fed up with these demonstrations that lead nowhere. They are not affecting the Jews in the slightest and are causing considerable harm to me who have, need I remind you, been entrusted by the Führer with the mission of preparing the country for war, because war will soon break out. In 1941 or 1942, at the latest, you can be sure of that. And we are still far from ready! The financial situation of the Reich is critical. We are lacking money, raw materials and manpower. And here we are: at the same time I am demanding that people throw nothing away, even empty toothpaste tubes, you, you are allowing entire shops filled with clothes, food and all kinds of goods to be destroyed by vandals! You might as well go the whole way now and set fire to the rarest of our raw materials! What criminal lunacy! If other such demonstrations, like your "Crystal Night", take place, I insist that they are at least managed in such a way as not to harm us, the Germans. Is that clear?

GOEBBELS

The assassination of our diplomat in Paris has enraged the German people. Public opinion considers this murder to be a demonstration of a global Jewish conspiracy against the Reich. The Germans know, as the Führer has told them, that thousands of men, who were sacrificed on the frontlines in the summer of 1915, could have been saved if only we had made 12 to 15 thousand Jews breathe poisoned gas. We would have won the war at once. People are extremely angry and the Führer does not want this anger to be turned against the government, like in November 1918. The people…

GÖRING

Don't take me for a fool! I know what you've done! We'll speak about this privately at another time. Do you know how much your "spontaneous demonstrations" have cost? In particular, do you know that when a Jewish shop is destroyed by demonstrators (*looking at the civil servants*) "justly indignant", when Jewish goods are thrown into the streets, German insurance companies compensate the Jews? And down to the last penny. Isn't that what you told me, Kehrl?

KEHRL

Yes, Marshal, that is what our insurers have told us.

VON KROSIGK (*tongue in cheek*)

That's what insurers have been saying since the creation of insurance companies.

HIMMLER (*tongue in cheek*)

Bravo!!

General murmuring

Incredible, isn't it??

GOEBBELS

When the people destroy a Jewish shop, the Jew is allegedly given damages by a German insurance company? Who says that? We can't let that happen! It's absurd!!! We must stop them! The Führer doesn't want that! The people wouldn't understand this.

GÖRING

And the people would be right! For once, I would like our propaganda -and you are still the Minister of Propaganda, are you not? - to do its job. I want it to make the people clearly understand that it is outrageous that German insurance companies suffer more from these demonstrations than the Jews themselves! What's more, I want to put an end to it all. In the decree I have just given you, it is clearly stated that Jews will not be compensated by the insurance companies for the damages caused during Crystal Night. This will show the people, once and for all, that things are changing. And in order to put all that into practice, I will need the support of each and every one of you, and of each one of your administrations, by following the correct hierarchical order. That means under my authority. *(Wörmann shows a sign)* Is that clear? Mr State Secretary for Foreign Affairs?

WÖRMANN

I do not see how a decree of this sort could be enacted. The insurance companies have signed contracts with their clients. They have no other choice than to respect their contracts and compensate the damages incurred by the insured!

Murmuring amongst the Nazis.

GOEBBELS

Why are you getting involved in this Mr Wörmann? This is an insurance affair and therefore internal. You should be dealing with our foreign interests instead! And finding a dumping ground to get rid of the Jews!

HIMMLER

You want us to reimburse the Jews, Mr Diplomat? I am surprised to see you leap to their defence...

Wörmann asks to speak.

HEYDRICH

Mr Wörmann should be careful. Criticism is only permitted for those who are not afraid of being sent to a concentration camp. And the law passed on April 7, 1933 concerning the "rehabilitation of the public service", driving non-Aryans away from their jobs, could also be applied to other people, even those sitting here in this room...

WÖRMANN

What do you mean by that? I'm not Jewish!

HEYDRICH

Anyone could be... if that's what we decide...

GÖRING

Be careful, Heydrich, that could lead to a very slippery slope... even for you... Mr Wörmann: We know that you have not been a member of the party for long. And we know as well that you are not one of our most... how should I put it? ... devoted friends at the Ministry... Furthermore, we do not see how insurance contracts with Jews could be of interest to the Ministry of Foreign Affairs.

HEYDRICH

It must undoubtedly be Mr Wörmann's personal initiative? Maybe he has a personal interest in this affair ?....

GÖRING

Heydrich! I told you not to go on about that. Mr Wörmann, answer the question.

WÖRMANN

I am speaking on my Ministry's behalf here, because the insurance issue puts our international relations into question.

GÖRING

Well then! In what way? Does anyone have a cigar? Kehrl! Go and ask for some cigars and have some coffee served.

Waiter moves about the room serving coffee.

WÖRMANN

Our insurance companies are mainly reinsured by foreign companies. When they compensate for damages, they are reimbursed by Swiss or American reinsurance companies. Our diplomacy ensures that the foreign companies reimburse our insurers when they should be reimbursed. But, of course, for our companies to receive this payment, compensation must be paid to the victims! Otherwise, we run the risk of our reinsurers refusing to reimburse our own damages and, in turn, refusing to further honour any other contracts they have with German companies if we fail to honour ours with the Jews.

GÖRING

I'm not so sure... I'm really not so sure ... In order to understand all of that a bit better I asked Mr Hilgard, Managing Director of the insurance company Allianz, and president of the Professional Association of Insurance Companies for the Reich, to join us. He's waiting outside.

He is best placed to inform us of the extent of the protection that our insurance companies have and the so-called restrictions that this imposes on us. I suggest we invite him in. He is not really one of us... In front of him, we will only speak of insurance matters. Is that clear? Just insurance!

ACT II

Hilgard enters, with an obvious Nazi salute.

GÖRING

Heil Hitler! Yes, yes... Hurry up. Sit down, Mr. Hilgard. Here, next to me. Yes that's it, Goebbels, make some space for him. *(Hilgard is sitting between Göring and Goebbels. Himmler, Heydrich and Daluege are on Göring's other side).* Our problem is the following: the day before yesterday the economy of the Reich suffered a number of... losses, smashed windows, damaged possessions, people hurt and buildings set on fire, due to the German population's anger against the Jews (which is entirely justified! Do you not agree?). The Germans wanted to inflict damage onto Jews (once again, in a justifiable act of defence!). And I am told that Jews could be compensated by your insurance companies? Be sure that they will not be compensated. If necessary, I can order you not to compensate them.

GOEBBELS

So, there's no problem. The Jews won't be compensated...

HIMMLER *(tongue in cheek to Goebbels)*

Does that put your mind at ease? It doesn't take you much to be…

GÖRING

Please, gentlemen! Calm down. The issue that is of most interest to me, and the reason why I have asked you to come, Mr Hilgard, is this: should these damages be guaranteed by foreign reinsurers, I would not like to give up what we could potentially gain from it.

(Hubbub in the room).

DALUEGE

He's clever.

GÖRING

I would like to talk about how to get hold of this extra currency, but rather than having it go to the Jews, how it could be put into the German economy instead? That's to say, to us. *(Göring looks at everyone with an air of satisfaction).* So, Mr Hilgard, do tell us, I suppose a large number of Jews are insured against the damage caused by "breaches of the peace"?

HILGARD

Yes, indeed. Almost all of them.

GOEBBELS

In other words, although our good fellow citizens, prompted by a fit of justified anger, intended to harm the Jews, your insurance companies, which are German, have the intention of giving the Jews a high rate of compensation, allowing them to re-do their lovely shop windows or to leave the country with our money? We cannot allow you to do that! Do you understand Mr Hilgard? Do you understand?

HILGARD

I understand. We have no choice but to do this. Our companies, that serve the Reich faithfully, also have duties to our shareholders. We cannot...

GÖRING

I can! All I have to do is issue this decree and there you go, it's magically done! You won't have to compensate them any more.

HILGARD

That's not possible, Marshal. Our industry functions on very old laws. It has lived through all the regimes, the Empire, the Republic and now the Reich. Whatever the regime, it will stand fast to unchanging principles, founded on trust. We have contracts with clients who pay their premiums. We are legally bound to compensate a client if the damage he has suffered is covered by the contract. Moreover, our insurance companies have signed reinsurance policies with foreign companies which reimburse us for part of the disputes: Jewish or not Jewish, these people are our clients.

Nothing but clients. We are not concerned by anything else. For us to do otherwise is out of the question.

Hubbub and discontent amongst the Nazis. The civil servants and the Minister of Finance are silent and very cautious.

HEYDRICH

Did you hear that gentlemen? "It is absolutely impossible". This clown is saying that just to annoy me. He wants to pay the Jews!!!

GÖRING *(very calmly, but in a threatening manner)*

You do realise, Mr Hilgard, that during my life I have done impossible things! Firstly as a fighter pilot during the war and then as the director of the first "rehabilitation centres"… A place for people who did not understand where their true interests lay… And I'm sure you understand very well where yours lie; do you not, Mr Hilgard? Yes, surely you do. So, we are going to look for a way out of compensating the Jews altogether, without losing the insurance benefits from these reinsurance policies, if that is alright with you? Very well. To begin with, Mr Hilgard, I would like you to tell me, in your opinion, precisely and to what extent the Jews are insured against the damage caused by a riot.

HILGARD

A riot is not covered by the insurance policies. However, in this case, it wasn't a riot! A riot is against the ruling power and no one was rising up against the government …

GOEBBELS

Indeed, if we look at it like that, it was not a riot (*with an air of irony*). Isn't that right, Heydrich? (*Bursts of laughter*). It was clearly against the Jews and only them....

GÖRING

If it were a riot, we wouldn't owe them anything?

HILGARD

Indeed. No insurance policy covers the damage caused by a riot any more.

GÖRING

No insurance policy covers riots "any more"? Did they *before*?... Are you saying that, for some time, you; by you, I mean the insurance companies, have stopped covering this type of risk?...

HILGARD

We have not covered anyone against the risk of riots since the beginning of the 1930's...

GÖRING

... You mean that you didn't compensate the victims affected by the damage caused by our various attempts to gain power, is that it?

Silence...

HIMMLER

Insurers always do whatever they can to avoid getting involved... And if this wasn't a riot, then what was it?

HILGARD

"Crowd movements".

GÖRING

That is the same thing. So therefore they are not insured! So they are not compensated!

HILGARD

They will be compensated because our clients are covered against such risks. (*Hubbub*) "Crowd movements" is not at all the same as "riots".

GOEBBELS

Well, it's simple; from now on you will not compensate for "crowd movements" either!

HILGARD

Contracts already exist. It cannot be decided in retrospect that they are not enforceable!

GÖRING

We can, if I want to.

HILGARD

No, we can't. Our companies have a name to uphold. And what's more, there's another problem...

GÖRING

What problem?...

HILGARD

The victims of these "crowd movements" are not just Jews and...

GÖRING *(he jolts)*

What do you mean, they are "not just Jews"?

HILGARD

...and I don't see how we could compensate some people and not the others.

GOEBBELS

Impossible! How so? According to the surveys that I demanded be carried out yesterday evening, the fire service did a very good job. The buildings next to the synagogues were only very slightly damaged. The non-Jews were not affected!

HILGARD

That depends on the type of damage.

GÖRING

Explain yourself Mr Hilgard, or do we need to drag words out of you?

HILGARD

There were, in fact, three types of damage, which are covered differently by our companies: fire, theft and glass breakage.

GOEBBELS

Ok, and so?

HILGARD

The Jews are the only victims of the fires in the synagogues because they are the owners.

GOEBBELS

Well! We won't give any compensation for that.

GÖRING

Let our insurance friend speak…

HILGARD

In terms of the shop thefts, the Jews are also victims, as they are the leaseholders of the businesses.

GOEBBELS

Very good! So that isn't a problem either. You see, Marshal, the insurers are…

HILGARD

… However, the situation is completely different for the glass breakage. The victims are the owners of the buildings. *(Silence. Solemn.)* But, the owners are mainly Aryan.

Hubbub

DALUEGE

You are saying that the Aryan owners will have to pay to replace Jewish shop windows?

HILGARD

Yes, General.

Angry mutterings…

GÖRING

Bravo, Goebbels! Bravo Heydrich! Bravo Himmler!

HEYDRICH

I stopped it from getting worse!

GÖRING

Daluege, you are Himmler's deputy, just like Heydrich. I know that you do not get on very well, but now you are in the same boat! Daluege, since June you have been organising huge raids in Berlin's cafés and avenues. Isn't your brother-in-law a police superintendent there?

DALUEGE

Yes, indeed, in Charlottenburg.

GÖRING

So you should know what the situation is. Do the Jews in Berlin own the four walls of their shops or are they simply leaseholders, as Mr Hilgard is suggesting?

DALUEGE

They are the owners! Take the department store "Israel" for example...

GÖRING

Ah!....

HILGARD

This building does indeed belong to a Jew. But he is somewhat of a special case.

DALUEGE

So it's the Jew who will pay for the broken windows!

HILGARD

Yes, but it is a special case. In general, the shop buildings belong to Aryans. The Jews are only renting them and so it is the owners who will have to repair everything!

GÖRING

Did you hear that Goebbels? Bravo!

GOEBBELS

It's not the end of the world. The owners will repair them and will then be compensated. That will create work for our glass factories, in particular those that we have just taken over on the Sudeten Land.

HILGARD *(giving Goebbels a hard stare)*

Suppose the glass needed for the shop windows is not made in sufficient quantities in Germany or Bohemia. Suppose it will have to be brought in from Belgium and will therefore have to be purchased using foreign currency.

Everyone starts yelling.

GÖRING

Foreign currency? And how much will this joke cost in terms of foreign currency, Sir, Minister of Finance?

VON KROSIGK

I don't have any estimates yet.

GÖRING

What a surprise, that would have been! Count, you have been Minister of Finance since 1932. We've kept you in this position because you are a so-called expert and you never know anything... Mr Hilgard, do you have an opinion?

HILGARD

I am reserving my judgement, your excellence, because I have only had one day to make the estimations... I would say approximately six million marks (*hubbub*), of which, half will have to be imported from Belgium and therefore bought using foreign currency. That is my opinion after an initial analysis. Even if certain specialists in this sector are more optimistic than I am.

KEHRL

Six million... That is a huge sum!

HILGARD

It is a considerable amount of money and what's more, as that represents half a year of production for all of the Belgian glass industry, it will take a long time.

KEHRL

And the Belgians will of course make us pay a high price for it!

GÖRING

That's enough to drive a person mad, to start pulling out hair and climbing the walls! Minister of Propaganda, you will have to explain that to the people!

GOEBBELS

That is impossible for the time being. This would turn against us.

GÖRING

I am not making you say it.

GOEBBELS

If you had let us take all of Czechoslovakia, instead of stopping us with your Munich agreements, we would have had all the glass we wanted!

GÖRING *(Very calmly)*

Be careful Dr Goebbels: the Munich agreements bear our Führer's signature... Alright, let's get back to insurance. The issue of the burnt down synagogues concerns strictly the Jews, so no compensation. The shop fronts, that concerns the Aryans; they will be compensated. And the third category of damages that you spoke about, what was it again?

HILGARD

Theft.

GÖRING

Ah yes, theft. Shouldn't this be considered more as "looting" during riots, and therefore non-insurable?

HILGARD

No, no, no! Once again, this was not a riot! Not one of the demonstrators was shouting hostile slogans against our Führer! It was clearly theft. A theft is characterised by someone entering someone else's property, forcing a safe, and taking something away. This is exactly the case here. Therefore we will compensate them.

GÖRING

It wasn't breaking and entering. It was a crowd destroying everything in their path and barging in during broad daylight!

HILGARD (*Still just as calmly, he corrects*)

It was theft. Admittedly with a brawl, but theft all the same.

GÖRING

No one broke into anything! It was hordes of people who ransacked everything. It was a "breach of the peace", so no compensation.

HILGARD

No, Marshal. Some people went into shops and left with what they had found! And Jewish shopkeepers are often insured against the risk of theft after "breaches of the peace"...

GOEBBELS

What? They can't insure themselves against riots any more, but they can still insure themselves against thefts after "breaches of the peace"?

HILGARD

Yes, this type of insurance still exists... Take "Marggraf" on Unter Den Linden street for example, it's not too far from here. Everyone knows this large jewellery shop? (*hubbub*) The owner, who is Jewish, has subscribed to a multi-risk policy with my company, Allianz, which covers all imaginable types of damages, including theft after breaches of the peace. The total cost of the damages reported to us is 1.7 million marks *(hubbub)* for this shop alone which was entirely emptied! We will, therefore, have to pay this.

GÖRING

1.7 million marks for one shop? They must have had treasures there? 1.7 million marks worth of jewellery! ... Stolen!! Disappeared.... These thefts are an outrage! Daluege, Heydrich, carry out raids across Berlin to find this jewellery! Daluege! Make use of your brother-in-law! I need that jewellery!

DALUEGE

I have already given out the orders! Passers-by are constantly being checked right across the city. According to our reports, 150 people have already been arrested for looting since yesterday afternoon.

GÖRING

But you haven't found the jewellery! It's not enough to check people on the street! These stolen items are probably already well hidden deep in basements. If someone tries to re-sell this jewellery that they pretend to have bought, without being able to prove it, you will have to confiscate it from them right there and then!... Have there been many thefts of this kind?

HEYDRICH

800 cases of looting in the country have already been reported.

GÖRING

800!...

GOEBBELS

Contrary to what we had planned...Eh, I mean "imagined".

HEYDRICH

We have already caught hold of hundreds of looters, and we are trying to get their spoils back... by making them talk...

GÖRING

Yes, the jewellery, the jewellery, the jewellery!

HIMMLER

They've certainly been thrown into the gutter by the rioters and then collected by other people.

GÖRING

Jewellery? In the gutters?

HEYDRICH

Children filled their pockets with it, for fun. The same thing happened at the furriers'! In Berlin, for example, on Friedrichstrasse in the 3rd district, a crowd gathered to collect mink, skunk, and all other sorts of furs! Ah yes, it's awful. The most precious furs and jewels will be hard to get back.

GÖRING

What a waste! Children stealing jewellery!...

VON KROSIGK *(Tongue in cheek)*

Today's youth isn't what it used to be.

GÖRING

We need to get all the police onto this!

DALUEGE

The Party could be very useful, for once! If the wife of a neighbour (everyone knows his neighbours) is wearing a new fur coat, or new rings, we can identify them. Reporting others should be made mandatory. We would like the Party to support us on this point.

GOEBBELS

We'll do it. And we already do it. Reporting people is absolutely obligatory.

GÖRING

Yes. Very well. Alright. We have to do it! The Party will do what's necessary. Let the Gestapo, SS, SD and the police work together for once! And you, Mr Hilgard, is this understood? You will not compensate the Jews. If need be, we will write all the relevant texts to cover you in terms of your foreign partners.

HILGARD

That isn't possible. We, the insurers, would like to be clear, Marshal. We do not want to be hindered with respect to our legal obligations to our clients, whether they are Jewish or not. The way you treat Jews is your business. That's another issue. But we must respect our international contracts and no Reich decree will free us from our obligations.

GÖRING

Forget your "obligations"! You only have obligations to your Führer.

HILGARD

It is in the Reich's interest that we keep our word. Our companies have a very significant international reputation and we have to make sure that the trust our foreign partners have in us is not put into question. Otherwise, our whole financial system will be put into question, and our currency along with it. If our currency collapses, we will no longer be able to pay for our imports.

GÖRING

Your established trust will not be put into question; from the moment I issue a decree that relieves you of your so-called "obligations". And defending our currency is not under your jurisdiction. This is perfectly well taken care of without your help, thank you.

FUNK

As Minister of the Economy, I am in charge of our currency.

HEYDRICH

If I could just say, Marshal, I am not an economist, nor a diplomat, but I do have a certain amount of experience in those things... In my opinion, we could let the insurance companies calculate the damage, compensate the so-called "victims" and respect their contracts, seeing as the insurance companies are so set on it...

Hubbub

DALUEGE (*muttering*)

It is the Jew Heydrich who's speaking!

HEYDRICH

....Once the insurance companies have paid the compensation to the Jews, we will confiscate it. This way, we will have allowed the insurance companies to save face and nothing goes to the Jews. Do you agree, Mr Hilgard?

HILGARD (*Totally changing his attitude*)

The solution suggested by General Heydrich sounds very good to me. The insurance company will check the existence of damages and compensate the person insured, whoever it is. Following this, what you decide to do with the Jews is no longer our concern. We are German, Aryan, and we only deal with the financial health of our companies, whatever the political regime...

HEYDRICH

Very well then.

GÖRING

Dear Heydrich... I knew you had certain talents, but I didn't know you took yourself for a magician. However, I don't agree with the solution that you have suggested. Mr Hilgard, you will not give any compensation to the Jews. None at all. What you should give to them, you will pay to the... Minister of Finance...

HILGARD

Ah, ha!!

GÖRING

... And what it will do with the money is not your concern.

HILGARD

That's impossible! We will reimburse the insured parties and nobody else. You do whatever you like with them afterwards, it is not our problem any more! It is legally impossible to do otherwise.

GÖRING

Legally… Of course, it's possible! All means, even those that do not conform to the principles of laws are legal if they serve the wishes of our Führer. Does that suit you? Mr Kehrl, as head of a business in the textile industry and in charge of economic issues within my Planning Bureau, you always have good ideas for these financial issues. This is the time to have one. How do you interpret this?

KEHRL

We could let the insurance companies compensate the Jews, as Heydrich is suggesting, and then demand that they pay a special tax, for example to punish them for plotting against us. Let's say a tax of 15% on their assets. According to my estimations, at this rate that will yield us a billion marks. With this money we can reimburse the money paid to the Jews back to the insurance companies, keep the surplus and we will have played our hand well.

GÖRING

I'll use your idea for a Jewish fortune tax. Very well. Well justified. But I do not want to let the insurance companies compensate the Jews. They will compensate the State. It's their job to pay for damages, not to choose the beneficiaries! Don't worry, Mr Hilgard, you will honour your commitments! (*Sniggering*). Mr Kehrl, is that alright with you?

KEHRL

I don't know, Marshal. Some companies (in particular the small ones that only insure for broken glass) will not have the means to compensate either the State or the Jews for the damages, and maybe not even the Aryans. In fact, all of these insurance companies for broken glass (except for one in Cologne) are small. If they are not covered by foreign reinsurance, they will go bankrupt... If they are reinsured, I do not see how to stop them from paying the Jews...

GÖRING

Mr Hilgard, are the insurance companies that have to compensate for broken glass reinsured?

HILGARD

No. There is only reinsurance for fire.

Murmuring

GÖRING

In other words, you are reinsured abroad for the damages suffered by the Jews, but not for those suffered by the Aryans? Bravo!

HILGARD

We didn't think that it was worthwhile getting reinsurance for glass breakage. Until today, no one had broken all of the shop fronts of all of the country's shops in one night... The "glass breakage" insurance was even one of our main sources of profit.

KEHRL

So you did put aside the funds to compensate policyholders?

HILGARD *(Very embarrassed)*

Not really.... You have to understand, the amount of damage caused that night is approximately twice as much as the total amount that we reimburse for all of the damage caused across a normal year. These compensation payments will therefore hinder our ability to make any profits.

HEYDRICH

We don't care about your profits! It's not really our problem! We have no interest in capitalist profits.

HILGARD

Excuse me, Sir, but it is essential for us. Look at the figures: the premiums that we collect for coverage against glass breakage are in the order of 6 to 7 million per year. Each year we compensate for around 5 million. This leaves us with a decent margin. I would even say that this makes us the most significant amount of profit. But now we have to compensate for 14 million marks, just for the night of November 9.

GÖRING

Wait a minute! Why are you saying 14 million, when it's usually 5 million and you said that "Crystal Night" was "twice as expensive"? Twice as much is ten million, not 14 million! Where do the 4 million extra go? What are you going to do with the extra?

HILGARD

We also have all different kinds of expenses!!! What's more, according to certain estimations, the glass breakage may in fact even cost significantly more than 10 or 14 million. That would make it 25 million, at the very least, which is 5 times the normal annual cost. It is really a catastrophe for us. I don't know how we will be able to pay, but we will pay all we owe.

GÖRING

You poor things! Complain if you will! If you continue to moan, we will nationalize you, is that what you want? How much do you estimate the damage to be, Mr Minister of Finance?

VON KROSIGK

I don't know. I wasn't there. Neither were my civil servants.

GÖRING

But of course, Count, you don't know…. I don't see why I'm still asking you questions… Mr Heydrich? Your men were very close at the time, they must have seen…

HEYDRICH

We estimate the total damage of the night (housing, furniture, consumer goods) to be in the hundreds of millions... (*Murmuring*). That also includes fiscal losses, taxes on sales, property and income, I am surprised *(sly smile)* that the Minister of Finance is not up-to-date on these estimations?

KROSIG

I still do not have any idea of the extent of the catastrophe as of yet.

GÖRING

This Crystal Night was entirely ludicrous! How many shops were affected ?

HILGARD

7,500. Including branch offices belonging to French Jews, such as Citroën or Etam on the Kurfürstendamm were destroyed.

WÖRMANN

Yes, and the French, they will need to be compensated, otherwise...

GÖRING

What a waste! Mr Himmler, your SS army should have intervened.

HIMMLER

And we did once we had received the order to do so. Beforehand, we did not make a move. As you know, we rarely bring out the SS. People are sick at the mere sight of black uniforms.

Krosigk asks to speak.

GÖRING

Mr Minister of Finance? Do you, for once, have anything to say?

KROSIGK

Another issue has been raised here that needs to be addressed. The majority of the products sold in these Jewish shops didn't belong to the shopkeepers, but to Aryan companies that had stored them there. These Aryan industrialists will not be paid, as their goods will not be sold. They will also incur losses. Are they insured?

HILGARD

Quite correct. These companies are paralyzed. They are, for the large part, insured. And we, the insurers, shall also have to pay for that!

GÖRING (*To Goebbels*)

What stupidity! I would have preferred that you killed 200 Jews rather than acknowledge such a waste of wealth.

HEYDRICH

91 Jews were killed! That's not so bad! We took great care to avoid such looting during the demonstrations. The looting that has been committed will be heavily repressed, however without prosecuting the ringleaders of the anti-Jew demonstrations.

GÖRING

Obviously. What will we do with the insurance companies that are unable to reimburse for damages? Kehrl?

KEHRL

Firstly, Marshall, I believe that our Ministry can perfectly decide, as you wished, not to reimburse the Jews under any circumstances. That's a first step.

GÖRING

Very Good. It's in the draft decree text. And what may be reimbursed by mistake to the Jews will have to be reimbursed by them. Like this, it will work perfectly.

KEHRL

Then we will see with each insurance company if it has the means to reimburse the Aryans and the State. This should bring the State, let's say, 20 million marks. We will come to an arrangement with the smaller companies.

HILGARD

20 million? We will never be able to pay that!...

GÖRING

If need be, we will nationalize your industry... even if that doesn't suit Mr Hilgard. The Budget will compensate those Aryans that could not be compensated by the insurance companies.

FUNK

The Budget, the Budget!! The Budget cannot cover the payments due by the insurance companies. The Budget must first and foremost finance the Wehrmacht. And as you know Marshal, the requirements for it will be huge in 1939. If the insurance companies are not able to pay for the Aryans' damages, we will drive these companies into bankruptcy and that's all there is to it.

GOEBBELS

We can't drive the German insurance companies into bankruptcy on account of the Jews!!!

Hilgard silently acquiesces, looking at Heydrich.

HEYDRICH

Everyone knows that Mr Goebbels' brother is at the head of Provinzial Insurance, a State company. He'd be very pleased if we nationalized the private companies.

KROSIGK

Furthermore, if the Jews pay a special tax, as Mr Kehrl so correctly suggested, the Budget will have enough money to help the insurance companies that are in difficulty.

GÖRING

... So, let me sum up. The insurance companies pay the State the compensation for the damages caused to the Jews' property for us to be able to first repair and then to resell it! Well, gentlemen, all this is very clear and we will adhere to it. For the time being, the companies represented here by the honourable, the very honourable, Mr Hilgard, say they are prepared to reimburse all of the damages. And I understand them perfectly; they want to give the impression that they are determined to do that, so that they are not blamed abroad for being unable to pay. And they will be paying out compensation, but to the State. That will cost them, according to Mr Kehrl's estimations, 20 million marks. This money will be more than welcome in the Budget. Furthermore, I'm not too concerned about these companies. If they haven't squandered all as dividends, they'll surely have the reserves to at least pay for the broken glass damage! After all, we're only talking about at least three or four times the premiums received in a normal year. It's not that bad. And if they are unable to do it, we should ask ourselves if it is wise to allow these companies to carry on. It may even be a mistake to allow these companies to exist. (*A threatening look is shot over to Hilgard*). This would amount to deceiving the people.

HILGARD

I am sorry, but...

GÖRING

And additionally, (I reiterate, additionally), the Jews will pay a tax to the State totalling one billion. Is that clear? For example, for Maggraf, the shop where all the jewellery disappeared, your insurance companies will indeed pay 1.7 million marks, but to the State! And additionally the owner will pay damages to the State to make amends for the murder in Paris. And if the police find the jewellery, it will also belong to the State. Regarding the food products that were thrown into the streets, stolen or burnt, there again, you will compensate, but you will pay the State, not the Jewish owner. They will have to pay the manufacturers for the products in stock that Count Von Krosigk was speaking about, just as if they had sold them. Indeed, in some way this is true. They did, how do you say?... "sell them off"!

Laughing.

HILGARD

The foreign insurance companies will protest against this embezzlement of compensation!

GOEBBELS

It doesn't have to be stipulated in the decree. We'll do it without saying anything. (Kehrl, don't take that down). *Göring signals to Kehrl to continue taking notes.* A general and vague ruling will largely suffice.

HILGARD

All American suppliers who deliver American furs insure them beforehand with an American insurance company, so they are covered. The international insurance companies won't be able to accept that we consider the looted marchandise as being sold.

GÖRING

I don't see how they could get involved in this and it will be clearly stated in the decree. The world should know what we are doing.

Finally, when all is said and done, your insurance companies will make a profit, as they won't have to compensate for all the damages.

HILGARD

How so?

GÖRING

Yes, you will not compensate the synagogues and all that! You should be delighted by that, Herr Hilgard!

HILGARD

I have no reason to be delighted. I am here to defend the interests of our German insurance companies, who are honourable Aryan merchants, and the interests of the insured Germans –Aryans– who will have to pay higher premiums, and I am here to defend the interests of German shareholders –also Aryans– who will receive less in dividends. The fact that we won't have to pay for all the damage does not mean that we will make a profit. I don't really see why not paying for part of the damages would be called a "profit".

GÖRING

Allow me to say! If you are legally bound to pay out 5 million marks and all of a sudden a guardian angel – assuming my somewhat bulky bodily form– appeared in front of you and said; I'll take care of four million and you pay for one million –for God's sake-! Isn't that a profit? ... Deep down, you'd like me to share it with you fifty-fifty, as the Americans say! Is that it? We just have to look at you to see that you are overjoyed, Herr Hilgard! Your whole body is smiling at the significant profits that are in line for you!

KEHRL

In reality, this gentleman hoped to pay nothing at all when he first arrived here. Neither to us nor to anyone else! He was sure that we would prevent him from compensating the Jews. He has slightly fought to pay them, but without really insisting on it. And now he is panicking because he can see that we have become aware of his excessive and unexpected profits, and that we do not have any intention of leaving them to him...

GÖRING

Yes! And Kehrl found you out! This is why I brought you with me Kehrl; you always have brilliant ideas about how to take money away from people!!!

HILGARD

If you do that, you will be penalizing all German savings holders, on whom our insurance companies will have to impose higher premiums, whilst at the same time we will have to pay fewer dividends to our shareholders. Aryans will be the main victims. That's just the way it is and it will remain so, and no one can tell me the contrary.

GÖRING (*Very angry*)

Well, if you don't want this type of inconvenience to happen to you, Mr Insurance Agent, see to it that there are fewer riots and broken shop windows! After all, you're part of the people! Send your representatives out to suggest to people that they break fewer windows!

General stupor and embarrassment after this ridiculous remark. Long silence.

GÖRING

Well, ok. Take leave of us now, Mr Hilgard. If you have any other questions, speak to Mr Kehrl, my assistant, who will answer them for you.

Hilgard leaves the meeting. Himmler makes a sign of annoyance in the direction of Hilgard to Daluege. Daluege responds by saying something to the effect of "I'll sort it out". Göring shakes his head in disagreement.

ACT III

FRICK

Those rotten democrats! They're still here, amidst the company owners.

GÖRING

The capitalists still haven't understood a thing. They pretend to obey us but they are actually the Reich's enemies. It's because we have respected their concept of the "law" and of the "word of honour" for too long that Germany is sinking.

Well, gentlemen, let's continue. We have both to get rid of the Jews and correct the mistake committed by yesterday's demonstrations. Read the draft decree that was handed out when you arrived (*silence as everyone reads*). Kehrl, you will add what we have just decided to the document... Any comments on this text? Mr Representative of the Minister of Foreign Affairs?

HEYDRICH

Him again? Why does he need to get involved! ...

WÖRMANN

Article 1 of the draft decree specifies that all Jews within the country are obliged to repair the damage incurred to their property during the riots.

GÖRING

Indeed. And ?

WÖRMANN

Foreign Jews seem to have the same obligation.

GÖRING

Indeed, that's obvious! Foreign Jews who live in Germany are bound by the same rules as the German Jews. Where is the problem?

WÖRMANN

Contrary to the German Jews, article 2 stipulates that foreign Jews should be compensated by their insurance companies. That's fine; it's what our ministry wanted. But they should also be explicitly excluded from article 1.

GÖRING

What do you mean? I don't understand your gibberish. And yet the text is clear.

WÖRMANN

Article 1 stipulates that "Jews within the country" - which includes foreign Jews currently in Germany – are obliged to repair the damages incurred to their property, even if they are not insured. Foreign Jews that may not be insured are therefore obliged to repair the damages they have incurred without being covered by insurance. Article 2 only covers those amongst them that are insured, and not foreign Jews that are not insured. They will consequently have to repair the damages at their own expense... We are likely to receive numerous complaints which will hinder our diplomatic position.

HEYDRICH

"Hinder our diplomatic position".... I must be dreaming!

GÖRING

Excuse me. I still don't understand. According to Article 2, foreigners will be compensated. What seems to be the problem?...

KROSIGK (*Whispering*)

The Marshall doesn't even understand the texts he has supposedly written.

WÖRMANN (*Patiently, with an air of commiseration*)

Foreign Jews will only be compensated if they are insured! If they aren't, they will, nonetheless, be obliged to repair the damages from their own pockets!

GÖRING

Oh, you're speaking of the foreign Jews that were not covered by insurance? I understand.

KROSIGK

Now he understands!

GÖRING

But they are few and far between! I don't see why this is a problem.

FUNK

Yes! It's a mere detail! Insignificant! They should have insured themselves!

HEYDRICH

However, I would like to raise a point of utmost importance. In this decree, an issue raised is the "confiscation of goods from Jews in order to finance repairs". We shouldn't mention the confiscation of the Jews' possessions. It's not worth displaying that in public!

Wörmann agrees.

GÖRING

No, no, no, it must be put down in black and white! We won't be able to do it without declaring it. We must establish a clear legal procedure. What exactly are you afraid of? Heydrich, are you afraid of going after the Jews?

GOEBBELS

That doesn't surprise me from Heydrich.... Much like you Marshall, I believe that we mustn't be afraid to tell the truth about what we are doing. Our Führer has been talking about seeing an end to the German Jews for fifteen years. Nobody believed him. Now that we have the means to do so, we must go ahead, without hiding.

KROSIGK

Mr Wörmann has pointed out a real problem. He is speaking about these foreign Jews without insurance who will all the same be obliged to repair the damages to their shops or their homes. This could indeed concern certain influential people and cause us grief from abroad.

WÖRMANN

Thank you Mr Minister. Indeed, we would need to face numerous complaints if we were to leave the text as it is.

GÖRING

Did you say "*influential people*", Mr Minister of Finance? I don't see what or who you could be referring to?? Listen, I'd rather not worry too much about foreign Jews, insured or not. Let's drop the issue; we have more important things to look into.

WÖRMANN

Well, that makes no sense! If Article 2 contains a clause that protects foreign Jews, then Article 1 should as well! I am sure that, much like myself, the Minister of Justice will want to protect foreign Jews.

GÖRING

Mr Minister of Justice, what do you think of that?

GÜRTNER

If I understood correctly, every Jew here is under the obligation to repair damages, yet only German Jews aren't to be reimbursed by their insurance company? Is that so?

GÖRING

It took you a while to understand! That is exactly what my decree stipulates.

GÜRTNER

I would like to know if anybody here is against the idea of also obliging foreign Jews to repair damages?

General murmuring

No, nobody!

GÜRTNER

As Minister of Justice, I do not see any reason why foreign Jews wouldn't be treated like the German ones. A Jew is a Jew. That's that.

GÖRING

Look here, Mr Diplomat! You are far too concerned with these people. And you, Mr Minister of the Interior, what do you think?

FRICK

Foreign Jews will have to repair damages, like the others, insured or not! In any case, to whom could he address his complaint?

Burst of laughter.

GÖRING

Rest assured he won't be able to. I'll make sure of that!

WÖRMANN

He could file a request for compensation to the German State.

Laughter.

GÜRTNER

By referring to which law? To receive compensation for damages caused by riots? We won't recognise the term "riot". We'll say it wasn't a riot. And indeed it wasn't. A riot is targeted against the State. That wasn't the case. As Minister of Justice I will affirm that to the whole world.

GÖRING

There you go! Bravo! Absolutely!

WÖRMANN

The international image of the Reich...

GÖRING

The international image of the Reich would be excellent, if you diplomats succeeded in convincing other countries to dispose of the curse of their Jews as bravely as we are disposing of the curse of ours. But seeing how pitiful you are, we must treat them as badly as possible, - foreign or not-, so that they decide to go and be hated elsewhere! Your foreign Jews will not only repair the damages to their shops, but we will also then take them away! Do understand Mr Diplomat: we hate foreign Jews as much as our own. Filthy Polish Jews legally stole our work, and we were supposed to treat them with complete honour? This has stopped. We have hunted them down.

WÖRKMANN

The agreement we concluded with the Polish government on this issue...

GÖRING

The Führer has annulled this agreement! He demands that you require the Poles to take back their Jews or to let us take care of them in our own way. The Poles dream of handing over their Jews to us in exchange for Danzig. We shall have Danzig and they will keep their Jews! From the moment a Jew has left Poland to come here, we no longer have any reason to treat him as a Pole! Indeed... (*Wörmann requests to speak*). Mr Wörmann? What is it still? I would like to put aside this business of foreign Jews and foreign policy for the moment. We have other, more urgent matters to deal with.

WÖRMANN

American Jews must be dealt with differently from Polish Jews... If we mistreat American Jews, the United States will take retaliatory measures against German goods in the United States. Thus, I am against this text.

GÖRING

Because there are still American Jews on the Reich's territory? That's news to me! Who are they then? The Warburgs! Felix? Max? Are these traitors still here? ... Heydrich?

HEYDRICH

Max is still here. And there are others...

FRICK

Max! The one who negotiated the shameful Treaty of Versailles on behalf of Germany, and who left everything to his brother Paul, who negotiated on the side of the Americans! We should have hanged him a long time ago for high treason!

GÖRING

I am fed up with the United States! German companies should liquidate their assets in the United States. That country of villains doesn't do honest business with us. The Americans took everything from us in 1918, just after the Jews –Luxembourg and Liebknecht and the others– stabbed us in the back. I don't understand how we can repeat the same mistake and trade with them again? And only for short-term profits! We can trade with serious countries, but not with one that attaches so little importance to the law as America. The other day, I was speaking to Hugh Wilson, the American ambassador in Berlin, about our magnificent airship, the "Hindenburg" which we reconstructed after its unfortunate accident... He maintained that it wouldn't be allowed to fly over America using hydrogen and that we would be obliged to buy helium from them if we wanted to land the airship in America. I told him: «*We don't need your helium! We will fly without helium and this splendid machine will only fly to civilized countries, where the law prevails. So it won't go to your country any more for America is a rogue country! Our Zeppelins will bear the swastika on their ailerons and will go around Europe to indoctrinate nations by broadcasting the military marches and speeches by loud-speaker from the sky.*" If you could only have seen the expression on his face, he was completely dumbfounded. A half-wit! It was good!... We should let the Americans know what we really think more often. It feels good...

WÖRMANN

I think that they have understood the core of our line of thought Marshall. This same American ambassador has informed me this morning that he was leaving Berlin! His government was very shocked by what had happened here the day before yesterday and recalled him. Mr Lindbergh, the Atlantic hero, our friend that you have just decorated with the Eagle Cross, and who decided to move to Berlin having bought a house here, has just given up. He is returning to America.

GÖRING

The Ministry of Foreign Affairs can be involved in issues concerning American, French, or English Jews; not Polish, nor any other Eastern European Jews, and obviously not the Austrians or Sudetes.

WÖRMANN

We want to be consulted about every foreign Jew, whatever their nationality.

GÖRING

Foreign Jews currently in the Reich will be treated in compliance with agreements passed in their respective countries...ah... if there are any? What's more, Jews that have always lived in Germany, and that have acquired foreign citizenship over the last year, just to protect themselves, must be treated as German Jews. I request that you do not grant them any special consideration! We have now finished with the issue of citizenship. Unless you still have any doubts?

WÖRMANN

I must insist. I would like the Ministry of Foreign Affairs to be involved in this discussion on citizenship. This is under our jurisdiction, and always has been. An internationally valid decision will be difficult to make without us.

GÜRTNER

"Internationally Valid" Pfff... We cannot consult you about every Jew, Mr Diplomat, but we will do it in general terms, out of principle!

GÖRING

Jews who have recently taken on another nationality are not your concern. If a Jew claims to be Czech in the Sudeten Land, we must not consider him as a foreigner; and the Ministry of Foreign Affairs will not be advised, because this kind of Jew belongs to us. In Austria or in the Sudeten Land, too many Jews have suddenly become English or American or who knows what else. Indeed, they will not be handled differently from the others. To be more precise, Jews who happen to be – or are yet to be – found on territories that are under – or yet to be under – our control will be handled as we handle the German Jews today. Did you hear me? That is to say they will be driven out of everything. And even more...

HIMMLER

I am not sure it is in our interest that they should go and join the growing numbers of our enemies...It is up to us to finish them off.

Goebbels requests to speak.

GÖRING

Yes, Mr Goebbels? Did you still want to talk about American Jews? The matter is closed!

GOEBBELS

Our diplomats should show our Western partners that an iron curtain has fallen in the East, and that we are defending the same ideas as they do against Stalin. You should make them understand that it is in their interest to help us face the Jews, who are slowing down our war efforts, so that we could join together to destroy the iron curtain.

GÜRTNER

As Mr Goebbels has so rightly said: an "iron curtain" has fallen between the West and the communist world and the Reich is on the front line to defend European values.

Funk asks to speak.

GÖRING

Yes? Mr Funk? Minister of the Economy? Do you have something to say about our foreign policy as well?

GOEBBELS

Stop making fun of him! Let him speak!

GÖRING

Ah yes, I forgot, it's your former deputy for propaganda, your protégé.... Mr Funk?

FUNK

No. I want to talk about some more concrete issues. What are we going to do with the land that the synagogues are on?

GÖRING

Land? What land?

FUNK

Now that the synagogues have been burned down, what are we going to do with the land that they were built on? Really, we can't leave it to the Jews!

GOEBBELS

Certain municipalities are thinking of setting up parks there. Others want to construct new buildings for the Party.

GÖRING

Excellent! How many synagogues burned down?

101.

GOEBBELS

Only one hundred and one? And yet it was, an ideal opportunity to get rid of all the synagogues in the Reich! All of those that remain standing should be razed to the ground! And by the Jews themselves!! At their cost. Anyhow, here, in Berlin, the Jews are prepared to do it. They tremble and do everything asked of them…. We will have parking spaces or buildings constructed in place of the synagogues. The same should be done across the country. The Jews should raze the synagogues to the ground and give us the spaces thus cleared.

General approval.

GÖRING

We will do it. Furthermore, I'm going to issue a decree applying to cultural law that will prevent Jews from entering theatres, cinemas and circuses. Our theatres are so full that there is hardly any space left for Aryans. It's unacceptable to see Jews sitting next to Aryans in cinemas and theatres. We could maybe grant Jews one or two cinemas in Berlin where they can see Jewish films? Potentially…. But they have no business in German theatres and cinemas.

HEYDRICH

We rub shoulders with them in the trains too. That too is unbearable! It must come to an end!

HIMMLER

Heydrich is quite right. Currently, a Jew can still share a wagon-lit compartment with a German! We need a decree from the Ministry of Communications for the Reich stipulating that separate compartments will be reserved for Jews and that they will only be available after all the Germans have procured a seat. If all of the compartments are full, the Jews will not be able to ask for a seat. The Jews must not mix with the Germans, and if there's no more space, they will have to stay in the corridor.

GÖRING

In that case, I think that it would be more sensible to give them separate compartments.

HIMMLER

Imagine that there are only two Jews on the train and that all the other compartments are full! That would mean that the Jews would have a compartment all to themselves to sprawl out? That's out of the question! Jews will only have the right to a seat if all the Germans already have a seat.

GÖRING

I don't agree! It would be better to reserve a compartment for the Jews! So that they don't mix with the Aryans, and if a situation, like the one you've just described, does arise, if the train is completely packed and there are Jews sitting comfortably in a compartment, believe me, we will not need a law to sort that out. We'll kick them out and they can cram themselves into the toilets for the whole journey!

GOEBBELS

There should also be a decree preventing Jews from making use of beaches. They invade our beaches! At Admiralspalast, revolting things have been happening recently. Just like on the Wansee lake beach, just near here. Wansee... Such a splendid place; it mustn't be polluted by the presence of Jews. We need a law to formally prevent Jews from basking in the sun on German beaches.

GÖRING

We could potentially reserve a beach for them....

GOEBBELS

Either we reserve one for them, the ugliest one, or they should be banned from the best so that we can't say that they're enjoying it. In the same way, Jews need to be prohibited from entering forests.

GÖRING

Ah, now that's very good! Mr Kehrl, forests are your responsibility. You should have an idea? ....

GÜRTNER

Doctor Goebbels is right. Great herds of Jews gravitate towards the Grünewald. It's a constant provocation and there are always incidents.

GOEBBELS

We have to drive them out! No more forests for the Jews!

GÖRING

On the other hand, we could arrange that a forest becomes a reserve for Jews. Kehrl, we could park them in the forests and let out all the animals that seem just as filthy as them, like the moose for example, with such hooked noses!

Bursts of laughing.

GOEBBELS

And the parks, the parks!!!! The Jews should not be allowed to sit in German parks. I'm particularly thinking of the public gardens in Berlin on Fherberliner Square. Jewish women sit there next to German mothers and their children. They gossip, criticize, complain and plot....

GÖRING

That could become very dangerous. It is imperative that certain public parks should be allocated to the Jews, the worst ones, and that they should be told "You can sit on these benches" with a sign stuck to the back of the bench saying: "Reserved for Jews".

GOEBBELS

Ah, and the Jews also shouldn't be allowed to do any business in German parks. The merry-go-rounds and the Jewish sweet shops; all that must come to an end!!!

HEYDRICH

And the schools! You know that despite initiatives taken here and there, Jewish children continue to go to school or university? It's unacceptable! It's out of the question that a German child should still sit next to a Jew in a German high school or that a Jew should go to a German history lesson or teach it! The Jews should completely disappear from German schools, pupils and teachers alike. They should take over their own education in their own communities.

HIMMLER

We also rub shoulders with their lawyers, doctors...and a whole range of other professions!

GÖRING

I recommend that we drive them out of all of the positions where they prove to be provocative. That is my criteria.

HEYDRICH

I suggest a further measure; take all the Jews' personal papers from them (their passes, driving licences.) They also shouldn't be allowed to drive any more, as they put Germans' lives in danger. Similarly, no Jew should be allowed to own a car. Their movements should be restricted. Certain places should be out of bounds to them. I'm specifically thinking of the Royale Square in Munich, by setting up fences and military barriers all around it with checkpoints. As Dr. Goebbels so rightly said, we must keep the Jews out of theatres and cinemas. Cultural activities and vacations are a "plus" that aren't entirely necessary. Many

Germans do not have the means to treat themselves to a session at a health resort. Consequently I do not see why Jews should have the right to go there.

GÖRING

To health resorts? I don't see why either!

HEYDRICH

And I would like to suggest the same thing for hospitals. A Jew should not be allowed to be treated in a German hospital next to a person of German blood.

GÖRING

Yes, yes, yes! We will have to manage that one gradually. All the same, we don't want them to transmit their illnesses to us! Aren't there already any sanatoriums and Jewish hospitals?

KEHRL

Are there any hospitals for Jews? Yes, Marshal, there are.

GÖRING

We will treat them only if they could be contagious to Aryans and that's that. Yes? Minister of the Economy?

FUNK

I would like to come back to Jewish shops. What are we going to do with them? We said that the Jews would repair the damages. Very well, but in real terms what will we do? It's Saturday today. Should these shops re-open on Monday? This is a decisive issue for us. The economy cannot function if all the shops remain closed.

GOEBBELS

The shops must re-open! They must be put back to normal as quickly as possible! Before Monday! And re-open. It's important for the morale of the population. People must find their shops open. I think that...

GÖRING

And if you want the shops to stay open so much, the best thing to have done, would have been not to wreck them. In terms of the question of when, how and with whom these shops should be re-opened, is for me to decide. In addition, the issue of Jewish shops is the main point in the decree that you have in front of you and I would like to thank Mr. Funk for bringing us back to the key issue. I was, however, going to come back to it. The way of dealing with this issue will entail dramatic consequences, yes, dramatic, which I have talked about at length with our Führer for two days and which we will have to contemplate in detail. The principle is simple: the Jews will have to hand over their businesses to the state, willingly or by force. All of their businesses. In exchange, they will annually receive a very small percentage of the value of their goods. They'll have to settle for that and clear out. That's the principle...

FUNK

That will take some time; filing, evaluating, compensating, finding buyers, re-opening shops. All that will create tremendous disarray at the end of the year, just at the time when our economy is cruelly lacking in factories to produce and shops to sell! Our economy will be in total disorder.

GOEBBELS

No! It's a blessing that we are able to close these shops selling frills and flounces. And Crystal Night has accelerated all of that. We have to concentrate on preparing for full-out war and only produce for the war! These riots are the opportunity to do that. Everything that was unnecessary has been destroyed.

GÖRING

Mr Goebbels, jewellery is not useless!!! And I don't need an economics lesson from you. You have done enough damage. Essential and very precious goods were destroyed the day before yesterday and their loss will be felt for the coming war. You have...you see, as I understand... The war economy is my responsibility; obviously it implies the aryanization of the economy. War cannot be waged if the economy is still partly in the hands of the Jews! The aryanization of the economy won't take too long, if it is carried out correctly. That's to say, by me. Methodically, with determination, cold-bloodedness. And brutality. We will never see the end of it with your civil servants from the Ministry of the Economy, Mr Funk. Furthermore, we have to make sure that nothing unreasonable is embarked upon in the lower ranks that would ruin our efforts (I'm particularly thinking of Governors and Gauleiters). No more demonstrations, anarchical despoilment, no more favours, no more corruption, no more pillaging for personal use! I'm going to immediately send out directives so that aryanization should be carried out methodically.

GOEBBELS

I'll see to that....

GÖRING

Just make sure that there are no more demonstrations of this kind. Playtime is over. We have to let grown-ups take over. (*He turns to the Minister of the Economy*) To answer Mr. Funk's question, no shop will be returned to the Jews. The shops that are not aryanized quickly will be closed. All these decisions will not be made by regional governors, but by us, in Berlin, because they touch on two key issues: the preparation for the war.

FUNK

This doesn't tell me if I have to plan the re-opening of Jewish shops for Monday.

GÖRING

There aren't any "Jewish" shops any more, Mr Funk! There are "shops in the process of aryanization". Before being the Minister of the Economy, you were Secretary of State for Propaganda. Therefore you should know the importance of words! From now on these shops belong to the people and nobody else. As Minister of the Economy, Mr Funk, you will determine which of the former Jewish shops have become useless. These shops will be excluded from the process of aryanization and closed immediately. After valuation, their merchandise will be sold to other shops at the State's benefit. The merchandise that cannot be sold will be given to the "Soup Kitchens" or other organizations of that kind.

FUNK

Should we compensate the Jews for the closure of their… of…these shops?

GÖRING

Mr Funk! Everything really does have to be spelled out to you! A State administrator, nominated by you, will estimate the value of the aryanized business and decide on how much the Jew is to be given. Naturally, this amount will be as small as possible and will only be paid out as an interest allowance, let's say 3 percent. The State representative will then sell these shops on to Aryans; at the highest possible price. The profits will come to us. Mr Minister of the Economy? Have you understood my instructions?

FUNK

Yes, Marshal. Just one more thing, who are we to sell to if several buyers offer the same price?

GÖRING

Good question. Priority goes to members of the Party on the condition that they are competent, deserving and efficient. Unlike some of your friends who hide behind figureheads! (*Murmuring*). Yes, yes, I know what I know (*murmuring*). Recently, some chauffeurs of Gauleiters have recently bought and sold Jewish goods so well that some of them, -or their bosses-, have earned more than half a million in just a few months! Gentlemen, you are perfectly aware of this. Isn't that right?

Embarrassed acceptances.

GÖRING

Minister of the Interior?

FRICK

In Bavaria, aryanization has already begun and is going very well. Compensation only represents 10% of the value of the goods. It's perfect and that can be easily explained! Fifteen years ago, when inflation was running wild, the Jews only paid under a tenth their true value. Therefore, there was no reason to buy the goods from them at a higher price!

GÖRING

You defend your underlings very well Mr Frick. But the reality isn't so simple. Indeed, let's have a look at what's happening in Bavaria! *He takes a file held on to by Kehrl, leafs through it, and reads...* Kehrl read the report we received this morning.

KEHRL

In Bavaria, public servants and notaries have been raking it in! The first aryanization contract dated from a couple of days ago – they didn't waste their time – concerns the purchase by the town of Fürth of all chattels belonging to its Jewish community! Goods estimated at 57,000 marks have been picked up for 100 marks. Very good. A second document states how the goods of a Jew, Salman, which were appraised at 1,800 marks, were purchased for 180 marks. Very good. The buyer, once again, was the town of Fürth;

but it was "represented" by public servants. This is where the scandal begins. In fact, these public servants were really representing themselves. Five notaries from Nuremberg and Fürth have alone received close to 100,000 marks in remuneration for having organised these kinds of transactions! Bavarian party members have just bought property worth 16 million for 2 million marks, bringing in a monthly revenue of 30 to 40,000 marks to the new owners! Would you like other examples? Streicher, Bavaria's Gauleiter, (everybody here knows him?) has even claimed that he was going to earn 30 million marks over the next six months in Franconia alone! For his own account! And he's not alone: his deputy, Vice-Gauleiter Holz just pocketed 1,578,000 marks from the sale of 38 Jewish houses; leaders of the Work Front, municipal councillors, lawyers, and even an astrologist, a certain Marie Obermeier, in charge of reading the horoscopes of these same men have also made fortunes with all of this!

GÖRING

Everybody in Germany is benefiting from the elimination of Jews; everybody but us. The money should have gone towards the State's budget in order to prepare for the wartime economy. Such things are unacceptable! It's high treason! I wouldn't hesitate to be merciless towards those responsible, whoever they may be! Should anyone of importance to the regime be involved in such dealings, I will consult the Führer myself within two hours! Be sure of that!

GÜRTNER

Yes, but is the priority to Party members to be upheld? It's what incites them to …

GÖRING

You are right: they mustn't have priorities unless they've got the required qualifications! That's to say, unless they've already worked in that field of activity; the buyers must know the trade of the shop being bought. Ah, and likewise: they must pay for it with their own funds, and not act as dummies for Party notables! Priority should be given to the oldest of Party members, and especially to those that have truly suffered to become one of us. For example, if one of our stationer friends in Austria has been deprived of his right to sell paper during the socialist rule because of his political beliefs, he should have priority in purchasing aryanized Jewish stationary shops. In other words, it must be handled as an ordinary sales transaction. A merchant (the State) sells; and somebody else (the Aryan) buys. The money then goes to the State and not to Party members.

HIMMLER

How would our stationer friend, whom you take as an example, manage if he didn't have the funds to buy the stationary shop? He might lose his priority. Why grant priorities if we don't give them the means to make use of them?

GOEBBELS

Himmler is right. In certain cases, our friends should be given help to make purchases!

GÖRING

No! No exceptions! This would lead to games with dummies claiming to be "without resources"! I'm sick of those people that see the Party as a means of getting rich! The Party isn't here to act as a social worker for imbeciles! The only Party members that shall be helped are those that have lost their shops following horrible chancellor Schuschnigg's decision in Austria or the Sudeteland. They'll have priority of purchase of shops in the Reich, and even be helped should they not have the necessary means at their disposal. They can even be granted loans in order to start up as easily as possible. But, all buyers will have to demonstrate a sales initiative, and buy the shops to run them and not to speculate. In these cases, the State will receive what was intended for the Jews, who shall receive nothing.

FUNK

With such priorities, the State will end up receiving less money! The budget for 1939 is already proving to be difficult to balance. Not to mention that of 1940...

GÖRING

There shall be no other exceptions. In all other cases, the sale shall have to be purely commercial. And party members will only have preference over other candidates if they have the same qualifications and funds. This should be put into place quickly.

FUNK

How many buyers can we hope to have? I need to know in order to anticipate revenues.

GÖRING

My services tell me that we should have around 60 Aryan candidates per 100 Jewish shops! Isn't that right, Kehrl?

KEHRL

Yes Marshall. That's what we can forecast today.

FUNK

Not more? Therefore, we won't be able to sell all of the shops?

GÖRING

We won't find a German buyer for every Jewish shop! Don't forget that trading is the Jews' natural activity, and that they owned 90% of German shops. Can you imagine! Hence, we will surely never find enough Aryan candidates to take on all of these shops. Especially now, when everyone in the Reich has found a job.

FUNK

What shall then be done with the shops that haven't found a buyer?

GÖRING

We close them down. Too bad, but we won't lower sales prices. And we won't wait to sell and to reopen them. We won't wait any longer. The war will not wait any longer. And the Jews will be an obstacle if it breaks out. Funk, you will nominate the special administrators who will oversee that all is moving along in order. Detailed responsibility will fall upon your regional representatives, and you will be responsible for their honesty.

FUNK

When do we start?

GOEBBELS

Straight away! People must understand that a visible change, extremely visible, is taking place and that the Jews are starting to disappear from the scene. They need to see that the country can go on without having to be obliged to come across the Jews on every street corner. That's what the Führer wants.

FUNK

An important point to bear in mind is to make sure that shops which have a Jewish name but already belong to Aryans are not aryanized. In all this haste, errors can be made. And some were made, on Crystal Night.

GÖRING

Does that exist?

FUNK

Yes, and quite a lot! Since 1933, Aryans have taken over Jewish shops, companies and banks. And some had the "bright idea" of keeping the shop under the Jewish name, as it seemed to have a "good brand image"! Can you imagine that?! Some of these shops or banks were ransacked the day before yesterday even though nothing more than their names were Jewish! We must avoid expropriating these shops.

GÖRING

Not at all! If they didn't want to run this risk, all they had to do was change the name! Aryanized companies should all change their names. I'll order them to do it! (*Discreet disapproval from Kehrl that irritates Göring*).... At the least they should add a German name before the Jewish one! (*Kehrl approves*). Funk, I am also asking you to take charge of the aryanization of shop chains and wholesalers.

FUNK

Excellent Marshal! I'll see to it.

HEYDRICH

And what will we do with the evicted Jews? On the street, and with no resources, they'll soon start causing problems.

GOEBBELS

Are you taking pity on them, Moses Heydrich?...

GÖRING (*Heydrich, bristles up, furious; Göring motions to him to keep quiet*)

Calm down! We will talk about that amongst ourselves a bit later on. Let's get back to the shops. Funk, you haven't answered my question. Can you open the shops on Monday?

FUNK

No. We won't be able to fix everything with a magic wand.... For a start, should we allow the Jewish shops that were not destroyed to re-open?

GÖRING

That depends on their turnover. If it is significant, that means that the German population is obliged to purchase their goods there as it would respond to a real demand. In this case, we have to let them re-open, even with their former Jewish shopkeepers. At least temporarily. If we closed these shops now just before Christmas we would experience a great deal of disorder across the country. Once again, I do not want the same thing to happen as in Bavaria where we transformed the aryanization of Jewish goods into a charity for incompetent Nazis!!! We have to move quickly, but in an orderly fashion. Mr Gauleiter from Austria, Herr Bürckel!

BÜRCKEL

Yes, Marshal?

GÖRING

You Austrians, who know better than anyone else how to deal with enslaved peoples, since Austria has been attached to the Reich, you seem to have understood how to deal with the Jewish issue very well. Tell us what you did to get rid of the Jewish shopkeepers so quickly without destroying their shops, like these imbeciles here did.

BÜRCKEL

Well, before the national revolution and Anschluss, we had prepared a plan. We analyzed the needs of each town, for each sector of activity and we selected the shops we wanted to keep, so that the Austrians wouldn't lack in anything. In Vienna, before Anschluss, there were 12,000 Jewish artisans and 5,000 Jewish shopkeepers. 10,000 artisans' workshops and 4,000 businesses are to be closed down. This will not interfere with the life of the Viennese. Only 3,000 out of the 17,000 businesses or workshops are to remain open and of course aryanized. That'll be more than enough. A law, written two months ago, authorises us to strike the artisans off the professional registers and to get rid of all visible traces of Jewish enterprise in Austria within the next six weeks... well, this is what we hope.

GÖRING

You hope? What could delay issuing this law?

BÜRCKEL

Negotiations between the Minister of Economic Affairs for the Reich and the Food Corporation have dragged on....

GÖRING

Once again it's your fault Mr Funk! ....

FUNK

The law is going to be issued in the course of the week.

BÜRCKEL

Once the law has been issued, closing the 10,000 shops will be nothing more than a formality. But afterwards, the merchandise will have to be recovered from these workshops and stores and that will be more complicated.

HEYDRICH

Everything must be taken! It's not that complicated.

BÜRCKEL

We need civil servants to do that and we don't have enough of them. Until last week, we more or less thought of letting the Jews liquidate their stocks themselves, but this won't be possible now, after what has happened in the Reich. The Jews cannot return to their shops on Monday, even to liquidate their stocks, even in Vienna. We are now thinking of creating a central agency in Vienna that will deal with the merchandise, check if it is still sellable, and resell it to Aryan shops, at a profit.

GÖRING

If I understand you correctly, you need to Aryanize 3,000 businesses and workshops in Vienna within a month. That's quite a lot. Do you think you'll find enough buyers for them?

BÜRCKEL

We have already selected buyers for approximately half of the shops; the deeds are almost finalized. For the other half, negotiations will no doubt be necessary and that will take some time...

GÖRING

What does that mean? That can't go on for over a month! May I remind you that we have to get rid of them as quickly as possible? The Jews must not be in our way whilst preparations for the war are being made!

BÜRCKEL

Ah well, if we don't find any buyers in a month, we will liquidate these shops as well, except for the shops that are absolutely essential, like some of the food retailers for example; they could then be managed by our men, civil servants from the Party. This would impact less than 100 shops. In any case, before the end of the year, we will have liquidated all the shops belonging to Jews; whilst the general public had never questioned their use until then.

GÖRING *(he looks at Kehrl, who approves and he claps)*

Bravo! That seems excellent to me. It's splendid. This will allow us to finish off with this saga by Christmas in Vienna, which has always been one of the Jewish bastions! We will be able to do just as much in Berlin and throughout Germany.... Mr Funk, how many Jewish shops are there in Germany?

DALUEGE *(laughing)*

The best estimation is that of the shops people found and destroyed yesterday: 7,500.

GÖRING

There are a lot more than that! Aren't there, Mr Minister of the Interior?

FRICK

Bürkel is hereby proving that we can perfectly resolve the Jewish issue by using rigorously legal methods. Our laws already exclude Jews from public service, medicine, and justice in order to protect the blood and honour of the Germans. We should do as much in industry. What's more, our laws have already defined "Jewish enterprise" for the last three months.

GÖRING

Mr Minister of the Economy, what can you do to carry this out?

FUNK

I'm going to devise an order that will prevent Jews, right across the Reich, from owning any retail, wholesale or mail order business. The order will close all artisan workshops from the January 1, 1939, which is in six weeks. They will also be prohibited from having employees, selling products on markets, accepting orders or managing a company, whatever type of business it is. Jews will not be able to belong to a cooperative and they will not be able to be an important executive in a private company either. All bosses must fire these Jewish executives within the next six weeks.

GÖRING

Very well, but can you explain to me why all of this, which was already anticipated in the law on the Organisation of National Work on January 20, 1934, has not been applied yet?

FUNK

It isn't so easy. It's not enough to just say that we are getting rid of them. They occupy key positions which are often very technical in companies, shops, banks, universities, hospitals and research laboratories. They are engineers, executives, teachers and doctors. Until now, we didn't have the Aryan executives to replace them.

GÖRING

Yes, but that's enough now! We cannot hang on to them. Especially those in strategic positions. Time is ticking on.

FUNK

In Germany in 1933 there were a total of 50,000 Jewish businesses; shops, industries, artisans and banks. Now there are only 9,000. The bulk of the work has been done.

GÖRING

Ah? As many as that? Shouldn't we copy what was done in Austria?

KEHRL

Yes, precisely. We should do exactly the same thing. It's perfect.

WÖRMANN

Complaints will be made...

GÖRING

Well, well, are you still here? All claims will be made in vain. Incidentally, the relevant Ministers are already authorized to act accordingly within the bounds of the 1934 law.

HEYDRICH *(Threateningly)*

I think that we can all agree with this text.

EVERYONE

Yes!!

GÖRING

In Germany, we will proceed vigorously, quickly and diligently like in Austria. There should be enough buyers to take over these shops before Christmas. The surplus merchandise will be distributed according to the procedure that you have suggested, Bürckel... Very well. Everything has been said on that subject. As far as I'm concerned, all of this preparation is excellent. Of course there will still be a few issues to sort out after January 1, 1939. We should be able to manage them using the same methods....

KEHRL

It should be easy for us to find buyers for these shops and at worst, if some are not bought, we will find tenants. There is a very high demand for that in Berlin.

GÖRING

Wait, no! My dear friend, if we were to do that, the Jews would get the rent money!!!

KEHRL

The rent would of course be very low. The Jews would surely accept an amount well below the real value.

GÖRING

A very small amount then! But this is just a temporary solution. I'd prefer we stick with aryanization, by paying the minimum. Mr Kehrl, couldn't the following situation happen: A Jew is aryanized and receives –let's say- 300,000 marks for it. Ok? He runs to the nearest jewellery shop, buys jewel upon jewel and disappears to other side of the border that same day.

KEHRL

We'll have to arrest him at the border and force him to return the jewellery! Anyway, even if the Jews earned a lot of money, they couldn't spend it! That's the beauty of the situation, they are trapped like rats.

GÖRING

How's that?

FRICK

They are required to make any changes to their financial situation known. If they earn money or if they lose it, they have to declare it. If they get compensation, they would neither be able to flee with it (as we won't give them foreign currency) nor would they be able to spend it. Therefore they cannot escape us.

GÖRING

But what if he nevertheless succeeds in hopping off with the money anyway?

BÜRCKEL

To avoid that in Austria, we spread out the payments to Jewish shops across long periods and deposit the money into a frozen account. The Jews do not have access to it and they cannot buy anything with it!

GÖRING

That's perfect. You palm them off by paying them peanuts! Excellent! We will do the same thing in Germany. Kehrl, note that down for the detailed procedure of the decree....

KEHRL

We could also stipulate that above a certain amount, payment will be given in Reich bonds or something equivalent.

GÖRING

Yes, excellent...we'll do that ...*Long silence*... But that's not enough. The Jews must give us back all the money that they have taken since they have been living with us. I would like to take up the idea that Kehrl had earlier and levy a specific tax for Jews to punish them for the assassination of Vom Rath.

BÜRCKEL

Yes. Like two years ago, when our comrade Wilhelm Gustloff was assassinated in Davos. Compensation was awarded to Germany for the damage caused.

GÖRING

And there was no need for a riot for that!!! Not like this time.

GOEBBELS

There was no riot because the Olympic Games were held in Berlin just after that. We had to make a good impression on everyone.

WÖRMANN

This is more necessary than ever today! The next Olympic Games in Helsinki in 1940 are looking bleak. Many countries want to exclude us from them. Our image abroad is getting more and more...

GÖRING

We don't care about the Olympic Games and the Finns! A Jewish wealth tax!... That'll bring us a lot!... Kehrl thought of one billion on a fortune of seven billion. How much do you estimate the wealth of the Jews to be in Austria?

BÜRCKEL

The Austrian Jews are not as rich as we had thought. Their industrial fortune is only at 320 million and the value of their apartments is at 500 million. What's more, we'd very much like aryanization to include residential buildings. (*General murmuring*).

GÖRING

You want us to buy up Jewish apartments? But with what money?

BÜRCKEL

Just with a virtual payment, fictively written into the Reich's budget and reduced by the special tax that they'll have to pay anyway!... Ah and I've also been thinking that it would be good, at least in Austria, to take all their bonds from them.

Another general murmuring, cries of surprise.

GÖRING

Bonds? You mean loans to companies?

BÜRCKEL

Yes, but to speak of this, I'd like it to be only amongst ourselves...

Göring assigns people to leave: Wörmann, Gürtner, and Frick. He then gives Bürckel the sign to continue.

ACT IV

BÜRCKEL

Do you realize that if anyone finds out that we are thinking of taking their shares from them, the Jews will flock to sell them at the stock exchange on Monday and it will collapse.

GÖRING

Ok, very well, we are listening.

BÜRCKEL

In Austria, a significant part of Jewish wealth, valued at 2.66 billion reichmarks, is invested in shares and bonds. This gives the Jews dangerous powers over our economy. They can ruin us when they want by selling their shares at any price. In my opinion, we should therefore confiscate them. And we can do it without jeopardizing the market. In exchange, we would give them what we would call "compensation shares" that would be recorded as a kind of virtual state debt. In reality, the Reich's finances would not be affected. The Ministry of Finance would only pay interest of 3% per year on this compensation over, let's say, thirty years and would obviously never reimburse it! That way, by retrieving the shares held by the Jews, the State would earn money because it would have neither to reimburse them nor to pay their interests. We would thus exchange real debt, - bonds and shares- for virtual debt. I addition, and above all, we would eradicate the threat of seeing the market collapse due to the sale of Jewish shares.

HEYDRICH

We aren't really going to pay interest to the Jews every year for thirty years!!!

GÖRING

I don't think they'll be here long enough to receive it!!!

Silence...

FUNK

I understand for the shares. It's ownership and we don't want them to own our companies, which I agree with! But bonds? Is that really necessary? They are lending us their money, it's all right? I don't see why we should deprive ourselves of that.

GÖRING

Because it's better to be paying only 3% for compensation to the Jews rather than 4% or 5% or more on interest for the bonds.

HIMMLER

Exactly! They make too much on the bonds. You should understand. Now look who's defending the Jews, Funk!

FUNK

Not at all. I entirely agree with Bürckel...Entirely...

GÖRING

Very well, very well. I'm convinced by the Austrian Gauleiter's argument. It is out of the question that the Jews keep their shares. They must give them back.... How much would the shares bring us Kehrl?

KEHRL

As an initial estimation, the Jews own about half a billion shares in all of Germany's largest companies.

GÖRING

Ah yes! Well... The State could keep them or sell them, depending on our needs.

BÜRCKEL

Not to mention that, in general, they are profitable businesses. The Minister of Finance can confirm that.

KROSIGK (*speaking haughtily*)

Admittedly, I can well imagine Mr. Bürckel's project, but we must realise that an entirely new situation will arise, one that is financially not very orthodox. The idea of taking shares from the Jews is very difficult to instigate and...

BÜRCKEL

Our policy will have no chance of being successful so long as the Jews have portfolios that they could quickly liquidate and make the stock exchange collapse in order to damage us or because they need the money or for any other reason.

GÖRING

You are quite right Bürckel. It's too risky. We should prevent the Jews from getting their money back and transforming it into jewellery that they can leave with!!

BÜRCKEL

Money that passes into Jewish hands should no longer be worth anything.

GÖRING

Very well! That's it, as everyone will understand that we'll never pay the Jews these compensation shares, they'll find nothing to buy with them! *(Laughing)*

BÜRCKEL

And that's that.

GÖRING

Perfect! They're really in for it. I wouldn't like to be a Jew in Germany at the moment... There are still many details to organise. What should we do with the seized shares? How do we manage the compensation? I suggest that a commission defines the details of the implementation of this idea; as of this afternoon, whilst the markets are still closed. I know that you'd all like to be on this commission! It will be at my Ministry so that it can be as small and discreet as possible.

FRICK

The Minister of the Interior should take part in it!

GÖRING

No, Mr Frick. Only my direct associates. Minister?

FRICK

Does the aryanization project also apply to Sudetenland?

GÖRING

Obviously! I hope that you have been listening carefully to what has been said here, so that you know exactly what must be done in this area! Of course, you should reinforce these economic decisions with police action and propaganda. Everything must be fine-tuned now in order to weaken the Jewish community from all sides at once... Mr Himmler?

HIMMLER

In order to have everything under control, Jews will need to be explicitly prohibited from investing their money into objects that they could hide, like paintings! In this way, we could be sure that they can't leave with them.

GÖRING

Yeah... But that would be too complicated and hard to check. Bürckel's idea is much better. We give them non-transferable compensation for their shares. The Jews will not be able to buy anything with it and they won't be able to do much with the 3% yield they'll receive. We will take care of the works of art that they already have in another way.

Heavy silence...

GÜRTNER

We're going to take their works of art from them? On what legal basis?

GÖRING

The Minister of Justice is starting to have legal scruples?... Very well... Mr Kehrl, having been the one who wrote this decree on my orders, tell us what is included in article 7...

KEHRL

"Jewish wealth should be put towards the development of the German economy within the framework of the four-year development plan".

Heavy silence…Laughing heard…

GÖRING

This article gives us all the means to put the excellent proposal made by Mr Bürckel into action. What's more, we should put it down in writing now; retrieve bonds, shares, apartments and all that… And in exchange, only leave the Jews with compensation certificates.

BÜRCKEL

I would also like a decision to be made on another issue, which we haven't spoken of until now; money borrowed by Aryans from Jews.

GÖRING

Yes, the bonds! We've just spoken about that.

BÜRCKEL

No, direct loans, loans of all kinds.

GÖRING

Ah, right! Aryans borrowed money from Jews?

BÜRCKEL

In Austria alone, the Aryans have borrowed 184 million reichsmarks from Jews. Can you imagine it! That must be the same in the rest of the Reich.

Discontent.

Heydrich

Loan sharks!!!

Bürckel

No, banks,... Jewish banks!! And, what's more, there are private loans, between parents or friends, in bastard families! Aryan artisans and bosses are subjected to Jewish creditors and that we do not want! Shouldn't we nominate government administrators to recover these debts and exchange them for compensation shares as well? That way, the debtors will no longer depend on Jewish creditors, but an Aryan trusteeship. The Jews will only be reimbursed when their due payments are settled! (*Laughing*).

Kehrl

Very well. But really, talking about that, even here, is taking a risk that it will leak out... I'm concerned that the Jews will start asking for their loans to be re-paid and start selling off their shares on Monday so that they can get money.

Funk

But what would they do with the money? Nothing. Having said that, it is true that if our discussions about the shares filter outside this room, there will be a run on the financial market as of Monday morning!

HIMMLER

No one will speak of it. Heydrich, make sure that all the people at this meeting are held to secrecy.

HEYDRICH

There's no need for any particular arrangement. We all know very well who says what, about everything... No one here will talk...

Long silence

GÖRING

I repeat, gentlemen, in your opinion, what would the situation be if I were to announce, on leaving this meeting, that a sum of one billion is to be claimed from the Jews, as punishment for their actions?

GÜRTNER

What actions? Ah, yes, I forgot the assassination of that Vom Rath in Paris!

Surprised silence ...

BÜRCKEL

The Viennese would entirely agree with this measure.

KROSIGK

Just one question, Mr Bürckel, can we create this tax without, at the same time, writing in the decree the ban on Jews selling their securities? The danger is that the Jews throw their shares onto the market to pay the tax!

BÜRCKEL

Actually, there's probably a danger there. The Minister of Finance is right.

GÖRING

How could a Jew bring his shares onto the market?

KROSIGK

By asking a bank to do it. That's the bank's job.

GÖRING

Well, I'll ban all banks from buying shares from Jews for the next three working days, the time it'll take us to take everything from them. Ah! Anyway, a simple decree could strictly order a ban on buying anything from a Jew. Anyone who buys shares, cars, jewellery or vegetables from a Jew will see these goods confiscated. I wouldn't set about it any other way. I'll do that! Yes, good... Note that down Kehrl!!

KEHRL

That can only be done through a decree.

GÖRING

Fine. Well, one decree more or less! Write it down! I'm asking you to get everything set up in the next three working days that means before next Wednesday.

BÜRCKEL

Three days? That's not much time! It may be the best way for us to put ourselves under pressure.

GÖRING

So it's decided. A fine of one billion marks will be inflicted on all German Jews for their crimes in addition to the 20 million from the insurers and the rest... I was thinking of formulating things publicly later on in the following way. Kehrl, where is the communiqué draft? Do it quickly! "The German Jewish community must pay the sum of a billion reichmarks as punishment for their hideous crimes, for disturbance of the peace at night (that's right "disturbance of the peace") and in order to repair the damage caused by justified national anger (blah and all that)". Will that be suitable? Those pigs won't commit any other crimes. Ah. I certainly wouldn't want to be Jewish in Germany! And what should I announce for the shares? Can I say that we are taking them?

General murmuring.

BÜRCKEL

Don't say anything! Above all do not say anything. Not before it has been done! Otherwise there will be a whole range of manoeuvres! May I suggest that we put the Jewish assets in a fund and we only let the Jews recover their compensation if our export revenue enables us to convert these amounts into foreign currency, so that they leave?

GÖRING

Well, children, have you thought about that properly? Did you not ask yourselves that this would cost us so much in hard currency for the Jews that in the end we would not be able to pay for our own expenditure? I don't see why we should give any of our foreign currency to the Jews.

BÜRCKEL

And yet we'll have to give them their compensation in foreign currency if we want them to leave.

GÖRING

Because it would be up to us to earn those foreign currencies for them through our exports. I have another use for our foreign currency, buying raw materials and oil is more important than providing the Jews with the means to lead a nice life elsewhere! And to strengthen our enemy.

KROSIGK

That's exactly the question that we have been asking since the beginning. If you take everything from them, if no country wants to take them in, if no one will pay for them to leave, how do you intend to get rid of them?

Another long silence…

DALUEGE

All that is too complicated...As for myself, if I were allowed to act...

Another long silence...

FUNK

There's also the issue of Jewish industrial companies to sort out.

GÖRING

The Minister of the Economy is right. We have to act quickly; given how worried the Aryan employees of these companies are, asking themselves if they will be unemployed next week. Two things must be clear, factories where production can be useful to us must be put into Aryan hands, just like the shops, and they will continue to work as they do today. As for the other factories, we'll suspend their production and see if we can convert them into something useful. I will need a lot of space and numerous factories. If we can't find another use for the factory, it will be razed to the ground. When a factory is converted or demolished, the first thing to do will be to check if the machinery can be re-used there or elsewhere. The companies' Aryan employees will have priority for immediate re-employment. We need labour, and keeping these people in their respective fields of expertise shouldn't cost us much.

BÜRCKEL

The aryanization of the factories will be a much more difficult task than the shops.

GÖRING

Why? These generally have only one owner and therefore no board of directors. A State administrator will take over the company that he will then sell to an Aryan or transfer it to the State. In the case where a large company, that belongs to many Jews or where the Jew manages it himself or with his sons, they'll have to be replaced with our own. The main thing is that maintaining production is essential and everything should work well.

Göring looks at the time insistently.

BÜRCKEL

The stock exchange is in danger of collapsing if what we're discussing here becomes public.

HEYDRICH

Stop worrying about that!

GÖRING

These issues are indeed extremely confidential. They should not be dealt with by regional authorities, but solely by me. The Gauleiters and the regional governors would of course be very pleased to hold the shares and to re-sell them and *"enrich our beautiful capitals"* with the money, bla, bla, bla… This is out of the question! I will be the only one to decide who these factories will be transferred to, and the only one to decide to what extent the State should keep them as they are, or to entrust its management to another State company. We should all agree on one clear procedure, which will be profitable to the Reich. This procedure will be applied to all shares held by the Jews and to all of their assets, which should be handed over to the German economy for the good of the Reich, without any preferential treatment.

KEHRL

We could bring them all together into one group, for example, like *"Göring industries"*?

GÖRING

Shut-up you idiot! This is not the place to talk about that! I have not yet thought about the details of the procedures. The main thing is that the Jew must be ousted as quickly as possible and that his goods should not be destroyed.

BÜRCKEL

We do indeed need clear and transparent procedures...

Goebbels

Exactly....

Long silence. Göring looks again at the time.

GÖRING

Thank you... The meeting is temporarily suspended. Goebbels, Himmler, Heydrich, stay here. Kehrl, you too of course. The rest of you, wait outside. I have to call the Führer to give him an update on our decisions. I will ask you to come back for the conclusions.

Everyone leaves. Daluege acts as if he were going to stay. Göring silently gives him the order to leave, under the triumphant gaze of Heydrich.

ACT V

GÖRING

Kehrl, ask for a line to Munich please. (*Kehrl goes and whispers into a telephone slightly further away*) We must stop showing our differences in public. You should accept my authority and stop standing up to me.

GOEBBELS

You're the one that hasn't stopped insulting me since the beginning of this meeting... There are limits you know!

GÖRING

I am not insulting you. I'm moderate, very moderate. Crystal Night was a mistake that you committed, you and you (*he points to the three others*)! A terrible mistake. If we don't recognize this, even our most loyal allies will turn against us. I do not want the Third Reich to finish in November 1938 in the same way the Second collapsed in 1918.

HIMMLER

No one will turn against us. People are too afraid...
Even if Crystal Night were a mistake, that you pushed us
to make, Goebbels.

GOEBBELS

It wasn't a mistake! Yesterday, the Führer had again
congratulated me. The nation was deprived of the fruits of
their labour by the Jews, deprived of its capital invested
abroad and of its colonies. The nation was right to act. We
mustn't fear the criticisms from foreign countries which have
been looting us for fifteen years.

HIMMLER

That wasn't the right way to do it! We are fighting an
alliance between the Jews, the Freemasons and the
communists. All of these forces that have been inspired by
the Jews are behind all the harm done to us. Our enemies
have figured out that if Germany and Italy aren't annihilated,
they will be. Hence, the Jews must be brought to an end. And
it isn't by demonstrating on the street that we'll achieve this.
Nor by our economic measures, but with a State-run,
methodical, and scientific form of anti-Semitism. The SS is
here for that. And without any sentimental feelings. I
gathered 30 SS generals in Munich three days ago in order
to develop our anti-Jewish plan of action. None of us even
thought of citing the attack in Paris, even though it took place
the same morning. We mustn't act on emotion, but
systematically. Even if there was much to say on the attack
in Paris...

GÖRING

What exactly are you insinuating?

HEYDRICH

Vom Rath was a close friend of this Jew. It's a private affair.

GÖRING

Where are you getting all of this from?

HIMMLER

I've got my sources.... In any case, this crime did not justify those riots.

GOEBBELS

Indeed, but you see, on the day of Vom Rath's death, at 9 pm, the Führer had ordered me not to interfere with the people's anger. A radical order.

HIMMLER

Yet, two hours later, the Führer asked me to stop the SS from taking part in the violence, and to order the Gestapo to ensure that the events didn't get out of hand, and to have 30,000 Jews arrested! And that's serious politics. The Jewish question must not depend on street rabble-rousers.

For Göring

That's enough! The Führer must not be used by some or by others just to justify your own decisions. Just two hours ago, he distinctly ordered me to stop your arguing, and to co-ordinate the elimination of the German Jews. And with all that's happened, it's me you are wronging. As if you were cutting off a piece of my own flesh! The Führer has given me ten years to rid Germany of them. Goebbels, unless you keep a low profile for a little while, it could all work out very badly for you, yes, very badly... As far as you're concerned, Himmler and Heydrich, bear in mind that you're just here to carry out my policies.

HIMMLER

We're only carrying out the Führer's policy. The SS took over power two days ago by not interfering with Crystal Night; and will not be letting go of it.

HEYDRICH

As far as I am concerned, I've had enough of the insinuations that I've been hearing here. "Moses Heydrich" ... I am not a Jew! My mother remarried a Jew! All of you here know that very well, as you've had an inquiry done on me in order to prevent me from getting promoted. I must add that we, at the SS, have a record of all Jews living in Germany. For example, we know that your Mother, Marshall Göring, had remarried a Jew, and that you have a half-brother and a half-sister who, therefore, are half-Jews themselves! As far as you're concerned Dr Goebbels, we know all about your sleeping around. And if you don't want your perfect family image to be torn to pieces, it would be in your interest to toe the line.

Long silence.

GÖRING

You have to stop that. None of us has anything to gain from it. We have a lot of things to do together. We must stop arguing. The Jewish issue is our joint responsibility...

HIMMLER

"Joint", if you may. But we, the police and the SS, are the ones carrying out the work.

HEYDRICH

And not only for economic affairs.

HIMMLER

... Because the economy won't be enough. The Jews can't stay any longer, wretchedly hanging about the streets in Germany. We must chase him out with increasing cruelty. We must be increasingly cruel. We're going to see to it.

GÖRING

The Führer gave me ten years to eliminate them from Germany. This is my responsibility.

HEYDRICH

Ten years! Can you imagine! At the current rate you'll never achieve that! We eliminate less that 30,000 Jews a year.

We were far more efficient over the last year in Vienna: thanks to the co-operation of the Ministry of the Economic Affairs, as well as that of foreign charity organisations, I have created a "Centre for Jewish Emigration" which had allowed us to expel 50,000 Jews in six months, whilst only 19,000 were expelled from the rest of the Reich during the same period of time!

GÖRING

Yeah, yeah, just for show! In fact, you co-operated with the locals in charge of the "Green border" just to achieve miniscule, yet spectacular expulsions.

HEYDRICH

This incident concerned but a small number, Herr Field-Marshal. Illegal emigration...

GÖRING

Your incident was covered by all the press! The first night, you expelled these Jews to Czechoslovakia. The following morning, the Czechs moved them along to Hungary, and from there they were sent back to Germany! And so on, from country to country. In the end, they ended up on a barge on the Danube. They're still there! Do you call that "expelling"?

HEYDRICH

This unfortunate incident concerned a mere hundred Jews. In reality, I organised the emigration of nearly 45,000 Jews... with a certain amount of damage I admit...

GÖRING

The damages aren't a big deal: when you plane something down, you're bound to leave some chips behind. And if we can't manage to make them leave quietly, we'll have to be done with them much more brutally, and if possible before the war! In the event of a war, they'll be in trouble, seriously in trouble. Our Führer told me yesterday: "If in the near future, the Reich is found to be involved in an international conflict, the world can rest assured that we, in Germany, will first and foremost think about fighting against the Jews".

HEYDRICH

The problem will come up even sooner as a result of the decisions that we've just made.

GÖRING

That is to say?

HEYDRICH

Well, aryanization, taxes, a ban on working, seizing their goods, will make paupers of them overnight. To put it another way, what will we do once we have rid them of everything, if we don't manage to make them leave the country as soon as possible? Will they become beggars hanging around on the streets? I would notably like to make some suggestions concerning the police on this subject, ones that are significant in terms of their psychological impact on public opinion.

GÖRING

That is to say?

HEYDRICH

Firstly, they have to be distinguishable from other citizens in order to apply a special treatment to them. The public must clearly see that they are Jews and that it isn't Aryans who are there without resources. Therefore I suggest that anyone considered Jewish by the Nuremberg laws wear an insignia. This should also make our relations with foreign Jews easier as this does not concern them.

GÖRING

Were you thinking of a uniform?

HEYDRICH

An insignia. That will be enough. A star for example. A yellow star... with six points.

HIMMLER

That won't be enough. We can't let them hang about the streets, without a penny on them! Even with a yellow star!

GOEBBELS

In Berlin, I personally managed to lock them up in a ghetto that they financed themselves, and that worked. But you didn't want us to continue with it, Marshal!

GÖRING

Yes, I put an end to it at the Führer's request.

HEYDRICH

And you were right. This ghetto had become a nest for criminals and terrorists!

GOEBBELS

My dear Heydrich, you cannot avoid creating ghettos on a large scale in all towns. They will inevitably be created to group all of these people together once they no longer have any work, or apartments, or anything.

HEYDRICH

We can't do that. The Jewish crime rate and terrorism would increase in the ghettos. They would serve as permanent hiding places for criminals and would be a breeding ground for epidemics. We certainly don't want Jews to live side by side with Germans, but having them under the watchful eye of the population is a far better solution than that of gathering thousands of them in a district where I couldn't get my men in uniform to properly control their everyday lives. As well, it would be difficult for me to entirely prevent Jews from communicating with those in other districts.

GÖRING

It would be enough to prohibit them from making long distance telephone calls! ... What if we were to put them into towns in which they would be the only inhabitants?

HEYDRICH

These towns would soon become havens for criminals of all types. They would become a terrible threat, gathering points for delinquents and enemies of the Reich.

GÖRING

All that will have to be sorted out. All of these issues must be resolved one after another. And if we can't, we'll get rid of them differently... Much like one throws outdated money into the fire... Kehrl, is that call coming? The Führer will be getting impatient. Alright, don't take any more notes, and let's speak of serious issues... Nobody must be able to confront us with text written by us on the matter. It is far better to meet rather than write to each other. No document must show that we have spoken of the physical elimination of Jews.

Silence.

HEYDRICH

The anti-Jew policies must no longer be in the hands of the civil servants. They are just pen pushers stuck to their seats. More than anything, they fear taking initiative. It's up to us to take on the elimination of the Jews with the army and the SS. The SS is able to act. We teach them to take initiative, freedom in orders.

GÖRING

In the army as well, they know how to anticipate our orders. It's the heritage of Prussian freedom. We don't have anything like that in the Civil Sevice. The army will help us get ridof the Jews.

GOEBBELS

I spoke about that at length with the Führer in Munich two days ago. He was preparing his speech for the sixth anniversary of the Reich in two months' time. He told me that the Jewish people often made fun of his prophecies and that he was once again preparing to be a prophet. He told me that if the international financial Jewry succeeded once again in throwing populations into a world war, the consequence would not be global servitude and Jewish victory, but their annihilation – *"annihilation"*; he definitely said the *"annihilation"* of the Jewish race in Europe. After that, I told him; *"The echoing laugh of Jewry would enter his throat"*. He said that it was a good phrase and that he would use it in his speech.

GÖRING *(He looks at his watch and then Kehrl, who is still near the telephone, and makes a sign of denial)*

As soon as the war starts, in one or two years, whatever the pretext, we will have a continent to run. We will have to control vast regions with a handful of men; regions where there are nine million Jews and we will then need to keep them out of the way in camps. In Siberia if possible, if not, then Poland.

HEYDRICH

In Poland? We'll come across three times more Jews there than here in Germany! What will we do with them? They're a burden of existence, just unproductive mouths. If we transfer them from one place to another, they will continue to be a burden. We have to settle this problem with an iron fist. The only solution to the problem of the Jews is complete annihilation, as the Führer said. That will also be the way to prevent the Jews from helping our enemies if they go abroad. I've always been against their leaving. And then their elimination will soon be forgotten. Who remembers the Armenian massacre today?

HIMMLER

The Führer asked me yesterday to send away to concentration camps as many fit Jews as the camps can hold. And Dachau has been filling up for the last two days.

GÖRING

How many people can these camps hold?

KEHRL

20,000 or 30,OOO at most.

HEYDRICH

We should build more of them.

GÖRING

One last thing, Heydrich. What do you think about the insurer?

HEYDRICH *(a vague gesture)*

People like him only think about protecting their fortunes, status, company, and pocket book. They think that the Reich is only a transitory thing and their companies will outlast us. So they kowtow, tolerate us, even join the Party, if it is of use to their career... They only respect fear. They don't know how to resist it. That Hilgard is ready to do anything to get contracts, to get a hold of aryanized markets, even if it means damning the Jews, delivering over his Jewish friends... In addition, he wrote to all the other insurers yesterday insisting that they don't take a different stand with us. It's a secret letter, so naturally I have a copy of it.

GOEBBELS

I don't like that man. I'm sure he will betray us.

HEYDRICH

Ah, he'd be on any side just to survive and to avoid the nationalization of Allianz. Upon arriving here at the Ministry this morning, he waited before coming in. He met some of your deputies, Marshal, who explained to him that Goebbels was in a very weak position and that it wouldn't take much to topple you, and that "we" would be very grateful. That is why he explained the consequences of the broken windows so clearly; so that he wouldn't have to compensate the Jews, and to please the Marshal, and to bring you down at the same time.

GOEBBELS

That's unacceptable!... Your associates, Marshal...

He also wrote another letter to the members of his federation, that he was planning on sending today and I have the rough copy of it here, where he explains that it is normal not to compensate the Jews, as opposed to what he defended in front of us here. He writes; "When an instigator is at the root of a crime, he is as guilty as the criminal. The Jews must therefore be treated as the guilty party in the eyes of the insurance company and all their requests must be considered as unjustified". You see, the defence of the Jews is not his main concern and you will see that he will do anything so that German insurers don't have to pay the 20 million marks in taxes that have just been decided.

The telephone rings… Everyone jumps. Kehrl picks up the telephone. He doesn't say anything, stands to attention and cautiously passes the telephone to Göring:

GÖRING

….Yes, my Führer. Yes, the meeting is almost over. I am with Goebbels, Himmler and Heydrich…. We have announced your decisions to the others without telling them that they came from you. The tax on the Jews, confiscation of their goods, no compensation for their shops, seizure of their jewellery and cars. We decided to seize their apartments, bonds and shares too… Yes that's it… Yes my Führer. We are also going to make them wear an insignia, a yellow star; so that it should be clear to everyone that only the Jews are destitute in the Reich…And then we are going to confine them to ghettos… Yes that could cause them to revolt… We're going to talk about it again. If we don't succeed in making them leave, we have no other choice...

We will need to get rid of them. The Jews will be a burden to us… They'll have to be annihilated, like you said to Goebbels. There won't be any more punches to be pulled. Yes my Führer… Yes… No we haven't spoken about that in detail… No we didn't take any notes. No, no, we didn't speak about it in front of the others… Yes my Führer… Very well… I'll tell them… Himmler and Heydrich? But? It's up to me to… Yes, no, my Führer. Goebbels?... You. I… Right, my Führer….

He passes the telephone to Goebbels then to Himmler who listens in silence without being able to get a word in edgeways and hang up. Silence…

GÖRING

Right, so I received confirmation of the assignment that has been given to me to work with you on the elimination of the Jews… from the economy. Goebbels, you stay with propaganda; you need to make sure that they are hated, but nothing else. Himmler and Heydrich…. Your responsibility is indeed to put the real solution to the Jewish issue into practice… Is that understood? Let's start working.

Silence. Goebbels has lost. Himmler and Heydrich have won.

GÖRING

Kehrl, bring the others back in and let's get back to today's issue. They must see that we are united. We must only show our common determination to get it over with. Where were we? Ah yes, we spoke about the Jews' goods, we must get back to their daily lives and make a decision about a last question: ghettos or no ghettos.

ACT VI

All the others re-enter the room and sit down whilst Göring continues to speak:

GÖRING

Come in, come in... Right, where were we? Ah, yes, the Jew's situation after we had him relinquish everything he took from us. So, if a Jew doesn't have a job any more, he'll have to live scantily; he can't get very far on 3%. That'll entail a concentration of Jews, which may make controls easier. We could call that a ghetto. We can't do anything else.

FUNK

The Jews will have to move within close proximity of one another. An isolated Jew, a solitary individual, will die of starvation.

GOEBBELS

The Jews won't have their own houses any more. They will have to stay in the hovels that we will leave for them. Even the richest of them, the doctors, lawyers, industrialists...

GÖRING

Yes!!! The ghettos will create themselves and we will also be witnessing a concentration of Jewish butchers, hairdressers and doctors in certain streets. And if we don't want to put up with that, the Jews will have to buy their staple goods from Aryans. That wouldn't be tolerated.

HEYDRICH

It would indeed be better if Germans wouldn't have to serve Jews!

GÖRING

And as you don't want them to die of hunger, (*wide smile)* the Jews will have to have retail outlets, where they can still buy their products.

FUNK

It's not at all what we want.

GÖRING

Except if whole districts or whole towns are reserved for Jews beforehand. Otherwise, as only Germans will be authorized to trade; Jews will have to buy their products from Germans.

HEYDRICH

So you want Germans to trade in the Jewish ghettos?

GÖRING

That's it, or leave the businesses to the Jews! I wish a decision would be made regarding this question just now. We can't say that this or that shop will be left to the Jews in the ghettos, which are bound to be formed, because once again, no control will be possible as these shops will work with wholesalers and we won't know what they're doing. Shops in the ghettos will therefore be run by Germans, but we will need to leave some jobs for the Jews. A German isn't really going to cut a Jew's hair! So some hairdressing salons should be run by Jews. But this won't apply to stores: there will be enough German shopkeepers who will have no problem with living in the ghettos, so long as they can trade there! (*Murmurs*). Enough! I'd rather Germans had Jews as customers instead of leaving the Jews to have their own shops, with German suppliers. And I wish the principle that the Jew must no longer have his say in the German economy would be applied rigorously. I will not go back on the decisions that were made earlier. You will give Aryans the right to move around certain streets in the ghettos and carry out certain tasks there.

HEYDRICH *(worryingly, threateningly)*

I do not wish to comment on this subject now, but I think that this will cause significant problems euh… from a…. how can I say… psychological point of view.

GÖRING

Once we have created these ghettos, we'll have to determine which shops should be there and be able to say *"You, Jew so and so and so and so, along with so and so and so and so, will*

deal with the delivery of goods to Aryan traders in the ghetto".
And a wholesale German company will be obliged to deliver
the goods to these shops in the ghetto.

KROSIGK

I would like to go further on Mr Heydrich's remarks. It
would be really... very embarrassing to have German
shopkeepers in Jewish ghettos. The very idea of a ghetto
doesn't seem at all worthwhile to me. Grouping Jews in
ghettos strike me as sheer madness. More generally speaking,
we shouldn't have to tolerate a Jewish proletariat in the
Reich. They will just cause us problems.

FRICK

Yes, Jews in ghettos will be a danger!

KROSIGK

The aim should be, as Mr. Heydrich was saying, to expel
all those that can be expelled.

Knowing stares between Göring, Heydrich and Himmler.

Silence.

GÖRING

Very well. Everything has been said. To sum up, we will use
the following communiqué *"The German Jewish community
must pay the sum of a billion reichmarks as punishment for
their hideous crimes, for breach of the peace at night and in*

order to repair the damages caused by justified national anger. The Jews must also refund all of their insurance compensation. The Jews must sell off their houses and companies. They will lose the right to drive. They will be concentrated in Jewish apartment blocks". Mr Minister of the Economy, you will be at the head of the commission that we have just set up and which will carry out all of the detailed measures that have been decided on today. There must be no escape route for the Jews. They won't know how to manage and they will have to pay anyway. They won't know straight away how much they will be taxed individually. Initially, they will not consider throwing anything onto the market. I know them; they will start chatting and then try to lay siege to your offices. Then they will visit all the powerful people over whom they think they might have some influence. They will go to the alleged *"Reich postal boxes"* where they will file their complaints. Some will even rush towards my office. You can imagine. All of this will take them time. Between now and then, we will be ready.

GOEBBELS

For the time being, the Jews are weak, hideous and are lying low at home. Now is the time to make a clean sweep and get it over with.

HEYDRICH

Get it over with.

GÖRING

I want this decree to be published quickly. This afternoon. For the moment, we have restored order, but who can guarantee that we won't have more riots this evening or tomorrow,

Sunday? Once and for all, I wish individual acts to be quelled. The Reich has the situation well under control and it'll see to it that Jews are eliminated...from the economy.

Everyone gets up in disorder. Murmuring.

DALUEGE

Marshal, can we issue the decree concerning the confiscation of cars immediately?

GÖRING

Check the details with the Minister of the Interior and the police. It's 14:40. This meeting is over.

While the actors come and bow to the audience one after the other, voice-over:

GÜRTNER

Died in Berlin in 1941 after legally justifying the extermination of Jews.

HEYDRICH

Appointed protector of the Reich in Bohemia-Moravia. Assassinated in Prague in March 1942.

BÜRCKEL

Becomes Gauleiter of Lorraine, a territory merged with the Saar-Palatinate. Commits suicide on September 28, 1944.

Göring

Sentenced to death at the first Nuremberg trial by the International Military Tribunal. Commits suicide in October 1946.

Himmler

Commits suicide as he was about to be captured in May 1945.

Frick

Sentenced to death by the international military Tribunal in October 1946; hanged.

Daluege

Succeeds Heydrich as protector of the Reich in Bohemia-Moravia. Sentenced to death in Prague; hanged in Czechoslovakia on October 23, 1946.

Stuckart

tried at the eleventh trial, like Wörmann and Krosigk, sentenced to time already served. Then appears before a denazification tribunal. Classed in the category of accessaries, fined 500 marks deductible from the amount of his pension. Paymaster in the town of Helmstedt, then head of the Board of economic promotion in Lower Saxony, dies in a car crash in 1953.

FUNK

Sentenced to life imprisonment by the International Military Tribunal; released on grounds of ill health, dies in his bed in 1960.

KROSIGK

Minister of Finance from 1932 until the end of the Reich; chancellor after Hitler's and Göring's deaths. Sentenced to ten years' imprisonment in 1946 at the eleventh denazification trial. In 1951, his sentence was reduced to time already served. He dies in Essen in 1977.

Wörmann

Sentenced to seven years' imprisonment by an American military tribunal; sentence reduced to five years, the count of aggression having been withdrawn. Dies in 1979.

HILGARD

Remains at the head of German insurance companies until 1945. Retires in 1946. Tried in 1949, fined 1,000 marks. From 1953 to 1960, chairs the consultative board of the Allianz group. Dies at home in 1982, at the age of ninety-eight.

KEHRL

Sentenced to fifteen years' imprisonment by an American military tribunal. Sentence reduced to time already served in 1951. Dies in Germany in 1984.

As the actors come and salute, one after another, we hear the off-scene voice:

FRICK

Sentenced to the death penalty at the International Military Tribunal in October 1946 and is hanged.

GÖRING

Sentenced to the death penalty in Nuremberg at the first International Military Tribunal trial. Commits suicide in 1945.

HIMMLER

Commits suicide whilst being captured in May 1945.

HEYDRICH

Appointed Reich Protector of Bohemia-Moravia. Assassinated in Prague in March 1942.

GÜRTNER

Dies in 1941 in Berlin after having legally justified the extermination of the Jews.

DALUEGE

Heydrich's successor for the position of Protector of the Reich in Bohemia-Moravia. Receives the death penalty in Prague and is hanged in Czechoslovakia on the October 23, 1946.

BÜRCKEL

Becomes Gauleiter of the Lorraine region, which is merged with the Saar-Palatinate territories. Commits suicide on the September 28, 1944.

FUNK

Sentenced to life imprisonment by the International Military Tribunal; released for health reasons in 1957. Dies in bed in 1960.

VON KROSIGK

Minister of Finance from 1932 until the end of the Reich, and Chancellor after the death of Hitler and Göring. Sentenced to ten years of prison in 1946 at the eleventh trial for denazification. In 1951, his sentence is reduced to time served. Dies in 1977 in Essen...

WÖRMANN

Sentenced to 7 years of prison by an American Military Tribunal. His sentence is reduced to 5 years after his conviction for aggression is withdrawn.

KEHRL

Sentenced to fifteen years of prison by an American Military Tribunal. His sentence is reduced to time served in 1951.

HILGARD

Remains at the head of the German insurance companies until 1945, then retires. Judged in 1949, he is given a 1000 Mark fine ... He dies at home in 1982, age 98.

TABLE

OTHER WORKS BY JACQUES ATTALI

After t he Crisis What is the future Fayard, 2009

From Cristal to smoke Fayard for French version, 2008

Ghandi a Biography 2007, Fayard, 2007

A Brief History of the Future, Fayard, 2006.

Karl Marx, biography, Fayard, 2005.

The Human Pathway, Fayard, 2004.

The Nomadic Man, Fayard, 2003.

Blaise Pascal: the French Genius, Fayard, 2000.

Noise, PUF, 1977, new edition Fayard, 2000.

Fraternity, Fayard, 1999.

Les Portes du Ciel, play, Fayard, 1999.

La Femme du menteur, novel, Fayard, 1999.

Atlantic Books, 1999.

Dictionary of the 21st Century, Fayard, 1998.

Labyrinth in Culture and Society: Pathways to Wisdom, English Translation, North

Beyond Nowhere, novel, Fayard, 1997.

Mémoires de sabliers, éditions de l'Amateur, 1997.

Verbatim II, Fayard, 1995.

Verbatim III, Fayard, 1995.

Manuel, l'enfant-rêve (illustrations by Philippe Druillet), Stock, 1995.

Europe(s), Fayard, 1994.

He Will Come, novel, Fayard, 1994.

The Economy of the Aapocalypse, Fayard, 1994.

Verbatim I, Fayard, 1993.

1492, Fayard, 1991.

Horizon Lines, Fayard, 1990.

The First Day After Me, novel, Fayard, 1990.

Eternal Life, novel, Fayard, 1989.

Literally and Metaphorically, Fayard,1988.

Sigmund Warburg: A Man of Influence, Fayard, 1985.

Fraser's Figure, Fayard, 1984.

A History of Time, Fayard, 1982.

The Three Worlds, Fayard, 1981.

Cannibalism and Civilization, Grasset, 1979.

The New French Economy, Flammarion, 1978.

The Word and the Tool, PUF, 1976.

An Anti-Economic Approach (with Marc Guillaume), PUF, 1975.

Political Models, PUF, 1974.

An Economic Analysis of Political Life, PUF, 1973.